Vishnu's Dream

Prelude

"There has been a technical hitch with the front wheel and there will be a few minutes delay while we wait for a pilot vehicle to tow us in." The captain's voice sounded confident over the intercom. Following a short delay the plane was towed across the runway. Passengers were soon walking across the tarmac breathing in unknown scents lingering in the evening air of Madras. Somewhere in the distance the Moslem call to prayer could be heard.

Dao and I offered our own prayers of thanks. We had arrived, in India, safely! And the pilot hadn't mentioned the "technical hitch" until well after touchdown. For us this was the start of an adventure, the culmination of plans which had begun long before we had ever met.

Ideas for the trip had begun in Thailand three years earlier with Gavin, "…a South African, from London." He was living in Bangkok and working as a sub-editor with The Nation. On weekends he would move out to recuperate in the clean air of Kanchanaburi 130 kilometers north-west of the capital. I was working as a private English teacher in Kanchanaburi and staying on a raft guest-house on the banks of the River Kwai. It was an ideal place to swim, laze in hammocks and discuss abstract notions.

We had both visited Calcutta and Bodh Gaya the previous year and had come into contact with Hindu and Buddhist thought. In Calcutta we had visited the Dakshineswar Temple to the north of the city where Ramakrishna, a 20th century Hindu saint from Bengal, had spent much of his life. "Few people realize that the purpose of life is to see God," he had said. In one sense it seemed to contradict the Buddhist view that there was no God, but that the purpose of life was to reach Nirvana. Still it seemed that neither God nor Nirvana could be described except in terms of The Infinite. These religious systems had evolved over thousands of years and had influenced civilizations in Asia throughout history. India was a land of variety, of ancient tradition often mixed incongruously with a modern world. Of cacophonic noise and intense peace, with a multitude of political opinions and social movements, where millions faced the daily struggle to survive amidst desperate poverty. Whatever the reason, religious or otherwise, we knew that one day we would have to return again to India.

At about that time an Englishman came travelling through Kanchanaburi by motorbike. He had shipped it from India and was planning to ride down to Singapore and then ship to Australia. The bike was a brand new, 350cc single cylinder, Enfield Bullet, weighing 185 kilogram's. The machine's reliable loud thumping sound told you it was coming a full 100 meters before it came into view. The Enfield's essential design had not changed since the original model had rolled off the production lines over fifty years before. That settled it. We would go to India and tour the land, visiting ashrams, temples and pilgrimage sites, by motorbike.

The next three years saw plans evolve, change, cancel, and become reinvented. As Gavin had never ridden a bike he thought he should learn. He bought a 250cc Yamaha Virago and a leather jacket. The leather jacket cost almost as much as the bike. Then he passed the most difficult of self-imposed driving tests by riding it around Bangkok for a year, without being knocked off.
I already had a bike, a road-trial 175cc Yamaha D.T. For no apparent reason vital parts would continually fall off it and onto the road. Usually it was parts of the exhaust-pipe or bits of mudguard, though a foot-peg, a battery cover, and then the battery itself, were all eventually lost. The final straw came when the accelerator cable broke causing the bike to rear up into a wheel-stand down the Bangkok-Kanchanaburi Highway. I began looking for another bike.

Shortly after that I met Dao. She was an accountant at the computer company where I taught English on weekends. *Dao* meaning "Star" was a nick-name considered too nice by her friends. More commonly she was called *Dum* meaning "Black" after her skin, which people found much more suitable. We both left the computer company a year later, but not before getting married.

Dao wasn't at all afraid of motorbikes. She had lived with them for most of her life, first as a passenger on her mother's lap, and later at the age of thirteen, as a rider. She even had her own one, a 110cc Honda Nova. It always started first time, and parts never fell off. While she was familiar with motorbikes she found it difficult to understand why anyone would wish to tour around on one in a strange country for an unknown period of time. Nonetheless she was, reservedly, prepared to give it a go.

A short time later Gavin went on a ten day silent meditation retreat at a Buddhist temple. He returned with Laxmi, "...a Gujurati from England." She had the well defined good looks of her Gujurati birthright and the quick wit and down to earth accent of an Essex upbringing. Laxmi was on holiday in Thailand and, despite having a great many family members in Gujurat, wasn't especially keen to join a motorbike expedition to go and visit them. She returned to England and Gavin left for Nepal. He would meet Dao and me in Madras in two months time at the beginning of January. We would buy bikes in Madras and from there set out across India.

A month later Gavin rang from Calcutta. He already had a motorbike. A 1991 model Enfield Bullet. He had bought it in Kathmandu and ridden it to Calcutta where he met Laxmi at the airport. She had decided to join the trip at the last minute. It was therefore finalized that the four of us would meet the following month in Madras. Dao and I would fly from Bangkok at the beginning of January while Gavin and Laxmi would arrive with their bike two weeks later, by train.

Chapter 1 Madras

January 6, 1998

"I live at my guru's ashram with my wife and two children," our auto-rickshaw driver told us as we sped over potholes the size of small craters. "Do you have a guru?" he asked.

"Ah, no I don't think so."

"My guru is also married. He has six children," he said, turning back from the front seat. "He is quite famous in these parts. But not too famous," he added. "Many people come to see him and receive peace."

It was dark by the time we had left the airport and found an auto-rickshaw driver in the car-park. He was a thin unshaven man. He wore a white cotton loongie around his waist and a white cotton button-up shirt, western-style with sleeves and a collar. Having agreed on a price for the journey he had disappeared around a corner and came back driving a yellow, battered, three-wheeled auto-rickshaw. He then took off his shirt and replaced it with an oil-stained khaki jacket. This, he told us, was his uniform without which, according to union rules, he would not be allowed to drive. We got in and the vehicle jolted forward not unlike a dodgem car in a funfair. Great mounds of rubble were stationed on street corners and in the middle of intersections and the driver chatted at ease while negotiating these obstacles great and small with the swing of his arms.

Given the word he would have taken us to meet his guru, but we had planned to spend our first night in India recuperating from the flight, at a hotel. This decision came about following a chance meeting with a hotel proprietor on the flight. He was a bright eyed man with a round face and a thick well groomed moustache. He had caught my eye in the corridor by way of showing the tip of his thumb pressed against his little finger. This I understood was to signal that he politely wished to gain my attention for a short while in order to detail the many advantages to be had by staying at his hotel. It seemed that he had also chanced to meet most of the other western tourists on that flight and we encountered them all once more, going in the opposite direction, when our auto-rickshaw turned into a small lane off Triplicane High Road and pulled up outside the Para Hotel. Small jolly children begged for money, biscuits or anything else that might be offered as we gathered our bags and walked inside.

"Ah ha! Welcome." The hotel proprietor greeted us. He was a large man with a broad smile. "We are full" he said, beaming with some inner satisfaction. That explained why the other tourists were going in the opposite direction. "But don't worry. In one hour some people will be checking out and you can have their room."

We spent the next hour chatting to the hotel staff watching cricket on T.V. in the foyer. They were all Catholics and all were related to one another, not that words were wasted on formalities.

"What is your opinion of Tendulkar?" asked one. "I think he's a fine batsman but unsuitable for captaincy."

"Yes you may be right," I replied.

"Of course Shane Warne is outstanding isn't he?" said another.

"Absolutely."

I tried to recall who was in the Australian cricket team and who they had played recently, but drew a blank. I hadn't followed cricket since the seventies, when Kapil Dev and Dennis Lillie used to square off against one another with little love lost.

As we sat discussing the finer points of cricket a constant flow of bare footed women in saris walked through the foyer and up the stairs. Each carried a high stack of bricks on her head balanced by a piece of cloth wound into a circle. They must have been very heavy. As each woman walked by she would touch her stomach and then lips with the tips of her fingers. Then she would open her palm while rolling her eyes upwards. Her other hand would be balancing the bricks. The whole gesture seemed to say I'm poor, exploited and hungry.

When the hour was up we were unexpectedly shown to a room. It was clean, brand new and sterile. All that would surely change given a few years to deteriorate. Dao loved it. Room service consisted of a boy, Raju, who ran for flasks of *chai* from a stand on the street corner. We took it. It was late but we had arrived, and India lay at our hotel doorstep waiting to be discovered.

The next morning we awoke to the sounds of bricks being dumped with gusto on our roof. The women began their day early.

"Raju," I called. The room service boy appeared. "Chai, my good fellow."

"Eight rupees," he replied. The going rate was normally three. Clearly the hotel had seized on a profit making racket. I gave him ten.

"Change?"

"Change is after coming," said Raju.

Raju returned a few minutes later with a full flask of hot chai, and no change. So began a steady relationship with Madras, and some of its inhabitants. Each morning bricks would be dumped on the roof and Raju would bring the chai. During the day we would catch up on the cricket scores with the men in the foyer and slowly begin to feel our way around amidst the noise and confusion of the neighbourhood. Two weeks later Gavin and Laxmi arrived.

Both were looking understandably dazed from from a forty-eight hour ordeal on the overnight mail from Puri. After the wild greetings we immediately ordered up two flasks of chai with Raju, who had walked in unannounced and was busy painting the room number in red on the bottom of the wastepaper basket. Then we got down to plans.

"As you've been here the longest you no doubt have a few ideas on which direction we should head off in," said Gavin.

"No," I said. "Laxmi you're from India so you should be the one to decide." All eyes turned to Laxmi.

"But I'm from Gujurat. This is my first time in the South and I know nothing about this region," she said with some pride. "My only hope is that we get as far as Gujurat before the bikes conk out."

Maps were unfolded, more chai ordered up, and talks went on late into the morning. Kathmandu would be the final destination but the possible routes to get there were endless. After further discussion it was concluded that as Nepal lay due north we would begin the journey there by heading for the ancient coastal town of Mahabalipurum, which lay sixty kilometers due south. From there we would move inland across Southern India to Goa on the east coast. If we made it to Goa we would rest up before turning our attention seriously north on routes to be decided when the time came.

"Before we go anywhere we need to buy a bike," said Dao. She had a point. That would have to be the first step. So far Dao and I had been in Madras for over two weeks and were yet to come across one that would remotely suit our needs.

The next day we happened upon a specialist Enfield mechanic named Aziz. He was covered in black oil as was everything else in his repair shop. He had a trim black moustache, black rimmed spectacles, and a friendly, untrustworthy grin. He pointed to a bare Enfield motorbike frame which had numerous other bits of motorbike lying scattered around it.

"Now is Ramadan and I am taking food only in the hours of darkness. Come back when it is all over and this machine will be ready to ride across India."

The Moslem month of Ramadan was indeed underway. Madras had a big Moslem population most of whom were fasting during the daylight hours. We retired to await the end of Ramadan.

The two day Hindu festival of Pongal was in the meantime getting underway. Its most visible sign was of yellow and red dots painted over itinerant cows, of which there were many. They wondered the streets gathering in contented groups to graze on great bales of grass specially provided for the occasion. It happened that during this festival Gavin commissioned some street children to wash his bike, covered in grime and dust from the long train journey. He returned later in the day to discover that while the bike was still covered in grime it had been dabbed all over with the yellow and red Pongal dots normally reserved for the cows. Gavin was greatly impressed and insisted on not washing the bike until months later when the last of the dots had worn off.

Two weeks later, on the last day of Ramadan a motorbike deal was finally struck with Aziz and come dusk the moment came to take possession of a 1988 model 350cc Enfield. As the design hadn't deviated significantly in fifty years it looked, to the untrained eye, exactly like all other Enfield Bullets. The one distinct difference with this particular machine was that the petrol tank, instead of being black, had been inexplicably painted silver by a previous owner. This had done nothing to improve its looks but would make it instantly recognizable in a crowded car-park. Fitted to the sides were two steel pannier frames where an assortment of bags would later be stowed. The handlebars had been adjusted to the correct angle. The saddle was large and firm. It felt reassuring to sit in it and be able to touch the ground with my toes, if only just, imagining that we were already out on the open road halfway across India.

"The clutch will take a little getting used to," said Aziz. He meant it was as good as it was going to get and it actually needed serious work. He smiled cheerfully.

"Thank you Aziz I'm sure I'll get the hang of it." Three attempts at the kick-starter produced no result. Three more, nothing. Aziz stepped forward. He muttered under his breath, curses perhaps, or charms, and the bike roared to life at his first attempt.

"It's just a knack," he said in his cunning, untrustworthy tone. His disarming grin helped him pull it off well.

"Goodbye Aziz," I said waving from the bike as it launched off into a busy stream of horn-beeping traffic. The time was six pm. It was just on dusk and Ramadan was now officially over. The streets were filling quickly with crowds of hungry, excitable people in festive mood.

The clutch seemed to be working well enough to change gears, but without ever fully disengaging the engine. This meant that the bike could never come to a complete standstill without cutting out. Considering the difficulty involved in restarting it, for this to happen would be unthinkable. The route back to the hotel involved a ride down Triplicane High Road which was now jammed with traffic moving at a snail's pace. Then all traffic came to a halt. There was only one alternative to stopping and stalling the bike and that was to follow the lead of a number of other bikes which were optimistically moving down the outside in the lane for the oncoming traffic. I followed. This seemed to work for about fifty yards until up ahead it became apparent why there were no oncoming vehicles. A bus was trying to turn left into our lane and was blocking all through traffic. In order to speed up the due process four *lathie*-wielding policemen were beating their thick canes against anything and anyone that happened to be in the way. The unfortunate motorcyclists whom I had followed were the main recipients of the brutality. The impending feeling that I was next on the hit-list sent a cool wave of consternation down my spine. There simply wasn't enough room to turn around and go back nor the time to attempt it before the policemen would be bearing down with their sticks. There was nothing to do but prepare for the oncoming wrath. Just when all hope seemed lost the engine cut out. I jumped off the bike and at the same moment, miraculously, a gap appeared in the teeming crowd on the footpath. I wheeled the bike up and disappeared safely into the crowd surging forward once more on it's irrepressible quest to celebrate the end of Ramadan.

Back at the relatively peaceful lane in front of the hotel the others had supposed that I had got lost and were not in the least surprised that I had turned up an hour later than expected. All came outside to examine the bike in its finally assembled condition.

"Do you think this crate will make it all the way to Nepal?" said Laxmi in mock amusement. The chances seemed slim given the difficulties encountered in riding the mile and a half from the mechanic's shop. Dao jumped up on the back seat to test it for comfort. That was where she would be viewing the countryside from for the next two-thousand miles if all went according to plan.

"Nice foot-rests," she said.

"Actually they're the pannier racks Dao," I explained. "The bags will go there. Your feet will be on those two rubber pegs." Dao hid her disappointment well. At least the seat was comfortable and the back wheel's suspension seemed to be holding out so far. The real test would be the next morning when the pannier racks would be loaded up with six heavy bags. There would be a huge rucksack of clothes and books on one side balanced by five smaller bags of assorted semi-useful things on the other. Everything would be held firmly in place with elastic straps. If any one of them snapped it would mean bags immediately spilling across the road. We tried not to dwell on that.

"Come on, we still have one last photo session to deal with at the Hotel Araati before leaving Madras," said Laxmi. She was right leaving Madras would be unthinkable without saying goodbye to the staff at the restaurant who had constantly attended upon us and supplied delicious food almost every day for the past month. The chef, Ramdas, who had personally supervised our cooking had insisted that we return for a last meal and photo session. He would be heart-broken if we didn't show.

We walked down the now hectic Triplicane High Road and up the ancient stone steps of the Hotel Araati where a prominent sign proclaimed "South Indian Veg Cuisine." The Hindu receptionist cum cashier smiled warmly and waved us in. He wore a large red dot on his forehead and had orange and yellow flowers sprinkled on his head. The overall effect was that of one having been standing under a flowering tree which someone had shaken vigorously.

The ceiling fans of the huge eating hall whirred just enough to keep flies from landing on them but not quite fast enough to affect the slightest whisper of a breeze on the diners below. Ram Babu, the aging head waiter, was clearly delighted to see us and showed us to a table with an air of panache. He took pride in his work and especially in his ability to predict what each guest would order. He therefore made it his habit to say out loud what each person was about to order based on what they had eaten the night before. A system which worked well if the guest regularly ordered the same thing. If not Ram Babu would always seem slightly disappointed.

This evening was to be different because, being our last night in Madras, Ramdas the chef would insist on our trying a taste from all of the tasty dishes which he had spent the day preparing. This caught Ram Babu out but if he was hurt he did well not to show it. Ramdas on the other hand was beaming.

"You have come at last!" he called out in a booming voice. The chief chef was clad in his usual flowing white cotton attire.

“Tonight you shall feast on veg kurma, rice, chappaties, dahl, aloo kofta, gobi 65, and mushroom soup.”

Ram Babu folded his little notebook and put it away. Then the feast began. Ramdas personally served each course, standing back expectantly as each dish was tried in turn.

“How is the veg kurma?” he would say. “It is perfect, isn’t it?” And, “I have added extra ghee to the dahl for better taste. Try some now it is Number One.”

The last course of soup was followed by three courses of sweets. Everything did taste very good to the delight of Ramdas who knew from the outset that it would.

“But where is your camera?” Ramdas turned with a look of almost tearful disbelief in his eyes. A photo session had been promised and he hadn’t forgotten. To his great relief I produced an instamatic camera from below the table. Pictures were taken aplenty. Staff photos on the front steps, chef photos in front of the kitchen, receptionist photos in front of the counter, waiter photos holding trays, and three group photos of everyone, taken by a passer by. The stranger looked like he had probably never used a camera before and treated it as an object of great awe and curiosity. Having taken the shots he wondered away looking slightly disappointed, realizing there was probably little to gain from the whole experience. He would have been correct had he been able to see the complete set of blurred and out of focus pictures that were finally developed. It was just as well that it wasn’t to be for at least two months and a thousand miles of road when we were long gone from Madras.

Chapter 2 Madras to Mahabalipurum

January 30, 1998

“Mahabalipurum is a town of great antiquity and charm. You will feel such peace there.” The chubby hotel receptionist rolled his eyes upward. He pressed thumb and index-finger together with an air of finality. We shook hands and bid farewell. Goodbyes and good lucks came from every direction as we staggered under the weight of the bags out onto the street.

Next began the complicated task of tying the bags to the pannier racks. Gavin and Laxmi had done this before and had it down to a fine art. They were packed and ready to go while Dao and I were still wondering how to fit everything in place. After twenty minutes of trial and error the bags were somehow strapped on. What didn’t fit into the bags: water bottles, towels, etc. were tied onto the lean bar at the back. We had packed six bags of varying sizes with essential and sundry equipment. The sundry appeared to outnumber the essential by five bags to one.

A goodbye committee spontaneously formed. We had been in Madras for over a month and our faces had become familiar with a number of the hotel staff and residents. Most were by now aware of our plans to ride to Nepal. There was the chai-boy, who always overcharged and forgot the change; the laundry man, who managed to have one serious argument every day with a dissatisfied customer; and the middle-aged men permanently watching cricket on T.V. in the hotel foyer. We never learned what they did when cricket wasn’t being played. On the street were the small happy children in rags. They begged by day and night and during the quiet spells played cards with the takings.

A dozen or so casual passers-by sensing excitement joined the party as Gavin kick-started his machine and the engine roared to life. Dao and I mounted our bike and tried to find comfortable positions amongst the luggage. Searching for some fitting words to say to those gathered I could find none, so I asked if anyone knew the way to Mahabalipurum.

“You are going to Mahabalipurum?” Came a voice from the crowd. An old man with a white mustache stepped forward. I recognised him as the man who always “Namaskared” to us in the street outside the hotel. His eyes were as bright as a young child’s.

“Yes,” I answered.

“It is easy to get to Mahabalipurum from here,” he said. “You just turn south at the coast road and go straight.”

It would be simple then. I thanked the man for his directions, said farewell to all present, and kicked down on the starter. Nothing happened. A few more attempts produced the same result. Three young men from the crowd took turns at fiddling with the carburetor and various other bits of the machine that should never be tampered with, before disclaiming all knowledge. Fifteen minutes later Gavin got it going to the great relief of the crowd, and the joy of one young bystander who claimed the success as his own.

Up until now the people in the crowd had been showing mute signs of boredom but couldn’t bring themselves to disperse. Some perhaps sensed this was the beginning of a great journey and too auspicious an event to pass by unnoticed. For others perhaps it was out of incredulity that anyone would consider undertaking such a journey that had to ask the way two minutes before leaving and couldn’t even get his motorbike started. Gavin and I drew up alongside each other, the thumping roar of engines drowning out all other sounds.

“This is it,” I yelled.

“If we get split up see you in Mahabalipurum,” Gavin called back. As pre-arranged we would meet at the Ramakrishna Lodge in Mahabalipurum if we lost one another on the road.

“O.K.” I yelled back. It seemed an uncomplicated plan.

Laxmi raised her thumbs. She looked comfortable surrounded by luggage on the back of the bike. Dao waved cheerfully and we all adjusted our plastic face visors. We rumbled away waving goodbye to all, down our small side lane and out onto Triplicane High Road heading for the coast. Showers of the night before had given way to a sunny afternoon with blue skies and occasional gusts of sea breeze. The traffic was busy, but at midday far from the chaotic grid-lock of rush-hour.

A short ride took us to the first landmark, the sprawling Madras University on Marina Drive. The years had done wonders for its charm with its main buildings slowly crumbling away. Now the vast blue expanse of the Indian Ocean came into view for the first time. The beach almost 200 yards wide was deserted but for the occasional fisherman venturing out across the hot sands. Here we turned right keeping glimpses of the ocean to our left. Mahabalipurum lay 60 kilometers due south. We would be there within two hours, if all went well.

It took some time to grow accustomed to the extra weight of the luggage and a pillion rider over the back wheel. The machine was now so loaded down at the back that the front tyre hardly seemed to touch the ground. It felt as though the first bump in the road would send the front wheel rising over our heads.

The engine still sounded reliable enough. Its deep trustworthy thump warned people within fifty yards to stand clear or be reckoned with. Before long it had taken us off in the wrong direction. A wrong turning at a fork in the road and we became totally lost. Gavin and Laxmi had ridden ahead on the correct road and were now out of sight. There were two possible routes to Mahabalipurum, the “old” road and “new” road. We had diverted from both and were soon discovering hinterland areas inhabited by farmers, cows and rice fields. The new route would turn the 60 kilometer trip down the coast into a 150 kilometer trial through uncharted fields and villages.

"Look at the green and beautiful countryside," said Dao, but I dared not look up. The roads were so uneven they were possibly built without the wheel in mind. We bumped down dusty, pot-holed roads, for many hours until eventually reaching a main thoroughfare with a sign saying, "Old Mahabalipurum Road".

A man cycled by wearing a Kashmiri costume of knee-length cotton shirt and baggy trousers. We recognised one another simultaneously. In Madras we had passed him every day for the past three weeks as he sat outside his Kashmiri artifacts shop. It was disturbing to consider how he might have arrived at this seemingly remote point on the Old Mahabalipurm Road. If he had cycled here it meant that the winding country tracks which we had spent the afternoon on had wound almost all the way back to Madras. We waved silently to one another and continued on.

We passed "Dizzy World," a huge amusement park with a long queue at the entrance, and a little while later a road sign eased our fears. It read "Mahabalipurum 15 Kilometers". On sight of this the bike engine, clearly obeying the laws of some higher force, cut out. We had stopped right in front of a chai shop. That was good enough. We stepped inside.

The chais and biscuits were served by a thin old man wearing just a cotton lungie. For all the business he was doing he might have opened his shop that day just for us.

"I don't suppose you get many customers out here," I said, noting there was no town and few houses nearby.

"You're the first today," he said. The time was 3.30 p.m.

"Then how do you ever make a profit?" I asked at the risk of sounding nosey.

"I don't," was his reply. Dao and I finished our tea pondering among ourselves the possible motives for running a non profitable chai shop.

"Is that sign correct?" I asked the chai shop man.

"It is," he replied.

"Then we are on the right road for Mahabalipurum?"

"Yes you are. It is 15 kilometers from this place."

The sign was not only correct but it was pointing the right direction. For some reason this took us by surprise. So accustomed had we grown to things not being as they first appeared that this actually seemed cause for congratulations. We thanked him for this welcome news, paid for the chais and biscuits and said goodbye. The goodbyes were premature. I spent the next ten minutes trying to start the bike without success. The chai shop owner's friend, quietly watching from afar, wondered over for a closer look. He started it on the second try. Dao and I thanked him and moved steadily off vowing to save future farewells for until after the bike had started.

The road was getting busier the closer we got to Mahabalipurum. A billboard featured a picture of a wheelchair with the caption, "Slow down or you may soon be changing your wheels." I slowed down. A little later the buildings of Mahabalipurum loomed ahead on the horizon.

"Dao. We're almost there," I called back. Shortly the town appeared on our right, and shortly after that it was disappearing behind us. We had passed right by it on the main road.

"Turn around," said Dao, "We've gone past it." We did a U-turn and found the exit.

Lo! Mahabalipurum! Ancient city of stone cutters and artists. We had arrived without having to change wheels. The Sun hung low on the horizon as we wound through a maze of back alleys and shuddered to a halt outside the Ramakrishna Lodge.

Bouganvillias flourished in the quadrangle and cool breezes blew in from the coast. Two heads appeared over the first floor balcony.

"We had narrowed your disappearance down to mechanical failure," said Gavin.

"Actually Gavin thought you had got lost," said Laxmi, "but given the simple directions we ruled that out as impossible."

"Lets discuss this over food," I said. We hadn't eaten since morning. Dao seconded that idea clutching an already half-empty jar of chili paste which her mother had made especially. She carried it as essential equipment on all outings to restaurants.

The four of us walked down to the nearby beach where an old hotel had a rooftop restaurant. Dao ordered a large fish and polished the whole thing off by herself. She was soon picking her teeth with its bones. Vegetarian food for the rest of us arrived. We ate, talked and listened to the roar of waves thundering down on the beach. The sea breeze picked up as evening closed in and stars began to shine. We returned to our hotel to dream of the road, of motorbikes, fields, oceans, and the roar of the waves and engines.

****

Dao and I awoke the next morning to a sea breeze blowing through the open window of our first floor room. With the breeze came the distinct chipping noises of stone carvers plying their trade. It was the sound for which Mahabalipurum was famous. The town had gained a name for its stone chippers back at the dawning of Hindu architecture and they had been chipping away ever since. Their seemingly endless supply of rocks hadn't dried up in over five thousand years.

From the vantage of the balcony we beheld the colourful view of comings and goings in the street below. A laundry man at the hotel entrance stood at a cart on wheels which served as an ironing board. His iron was heated by a built-in charcoal fire which he blew on occasionally to keep it stoked. Across the road a woman's head appeared over a wall. She was having a morning bath and quickly emptied half-a-dozen buckets of water over herself. Just then a tall man with a long white beard came walking down the opposite side-alley.

"Look at that man," said Dao. "He's looking over the wall at that woman having a bath." He did appear to be staring at her. Just then he continued around the corner onto our road tapping a stick and nearly bumped into the laundry cart. He was blind. The woman herself then opened a side door and stepped out onto the street. She was fully covered wearing a wet sarong.

We decided to join Gavin and Laxmi on an early morning walk along the beach. Waves were being whipped up to white caps by a gusty breeze and dozens of fishermen's rafts were pulled up on the sand. Each raft was made of a number of great lengths of carved wood lashed together with nothing but pieces of rope at each end. Even the smallest of waves would wash over their decks yet they were designed to stay afloat in any storm. Long wooden masts lay on the decks with sails neatly stowed.

"Shall we ask the fisherman if they'll take us out one morning?" I asked Dao.

"No," she replied. "The weather's too unpredictable and the waves look dangerous."

She was probably right. Generations of fishermen had been lost at sea off this coast. Looking out to sea wild waves could be seen rolling in and crashing onto the beach. They were accompanied by a stiff cool breeze.

Despite the prevailing conditions Gavin, Laxmi and I decided on an early morning swim. It would be just the thing to wake us up and help gain an appetite for breakfast. Dao, wisely in hindsight, chose not to. Gavin and I swam out past the breakers twenty meters off the coast. One meter waves rolled in steadily without apparent danger. Suddenly Laxmi began to call out for help. A damsel in distress! As she was in close to the shore it would present little difficulty rushing to her aid. Gavin being the stronger swimmer reached Laxmi first. He had already carried her out of the water by the time I reached the spot. Then I understood why Laxmi had called out. It was the point of two converging wave patterns causing an undertow, making it very difficult to reach the beach. For about five minutes I tried without success and was starting to get breathless. Gavin stood on the beach about ten yards away calling out to ask if I needed help. That would be an indignity, "The rescuer gets rescued!" I waved my arm in a half-hearted show of being OK and then tried swimming parallel to the coast until getting past the danger spot. A few minutes later I was back on the beach feeling washed up and happy to be alive. A Buddha medal which had hung around my neck was gone, consigned to the waves. The sea gods had spared us, but not without issuing a small reminder of man's mortality. It was probably good for the soul to have such reminders from time to time. In the coming few months on the road we would be receiving more than usual.

The next two days were spent walking from rocky pillar to post taking in some of the town's historic atmosphere. Stone carvings, temples and hand-cut caves dated back over a thousand years. Among them the ancient Shore Temple stood magnificently on the high point of a promontory overlooking the sea. From south to north stretched a continuous white sandy beach. The temple was over twelve hundred years old. Its main shrine housed an ancient reclining Vishnu cut from stone. The steady sound of waves crashing on the beach seemed to be paying continuous homage to the Lord of the Universe eternally at peace with creation. Nothing happens by accident in Vishnu's world. All is ordained according to patterns which we weave for ourselves without ever really understanding their consequences even as they ripen. The message, it seemed to me, was to trust in the Absolute, to observe, to act, but to maintain supreme non-attachment to the outer circumstances of one's life. Then all would unfold as it should. All would be discovered as spirit and truth, one in the mind of Vishnu. Ancient sites where people have stopped to worship and meditate since time immemorial offen take on a healing vibration of peace which many attest to but few can explain. India was full of such places. They seemed to act by way of compensation for the never ending hustle and bustle of normal daily life. I left that place with a strong sense of peace as we walked east out of the temple grounds down a noisy row of souvenir shops selling all manner of stone carvings and trinkets.

Hello sir, shaving?" A bald, unshaven man called out from a barber's shop. He was presumably a barber. I stepped inside and was ushered to sit down on perhaps the first ever model design of a barber's chair. Sinking into its forgiving springs the leather upholstery wraps around and holds one firmly in its grasp. One's feet rest at an incline a foot higher than necessary while, as there is no headrest, one's head rolls over the back of the chair leaving one to gaze helplessly upside down at pictures of Hindu deities on the back wall. More than thirty seconds in this position would be uncomfortable. The grinning, chatty barber spent five minutes lathering up my chin.

"How are you feeling in our Mahabalipurum?" he asked, slapping foam across my stretched neck, under my nose and across tightly pursed lips. I had no intention of risking a mouthful of foam to answer. He pinched my nostrils shut to avoid foam shooting up them with each inhalation. The only alternative to suffocation was to draw in long steady breaths through the corners of my mouth.

"Mahabalipurum's fine!" I spurted out on the out breath, sending up a fine spray of foamy bubbles.

"Yes. It is world famous," he said, beaming. "Have you seen Arjuna's Penance?" He referred to the huge bass-relief rock carving located in the centre of town. A blind man couldn't have missed it. I was suffering my own little penance just then.

"Yes I have," I uttered before foam dribbled into my mouth.

"It's a masterpiece," he added. "May I enquire your good name?" I gave my name. "And native place?" I gave my native place. Out came the new blade into the cut-throat razor handle. The point of no return.

"What is your cast?" he asked.

"I am a teacher," I said, unsure if that constituted caste.

"Ah! You are a school master. A noble profession," he said with genuine admiration. He chatted continually, smiling all the time and taking great pride in his work. Ten minutes later I was standing up feeling clean shaven and respectable. My neck muscles had contracted into a semi-permanent state of fixation whereby I could only gaze upwards.

"What is your next programme?" asked the barber as we stepped outside together.

"Vedangtangal," I said.

"Vedangtangal? It is a bird sanctuary." The barber held both hands palms upward and beamed. "You will witness the most extraordinary display of water birds from every quarter filling the sky at once."

Stepping out on to the street with strained neck and eyes gazing up, I felt that walking back to the hotel was going to be dangerous. It would be ideal for bird watching. But it was still a long way to Vedangtangal.

Chapter 3 Mahabalipurum to Vedangtangal

February 3, 1998

“You are going to Vedangtangal?” A thin old man sitting down on the bench opposite had asked. Gavin, Laxmi, Dao and I had been discussing plans over chai at a small open-air chai stall. It was situated on the corner of two fairly busy roads and was always sure to be doing a brisk trade.

“Yes,” said Gavin in a matter-of-fact way, not really wishing to be disturbed.

“It lies forty-five kilometers east of this place,” said the old man.

“So I understand,” said Gavin being patient.

“It is a bird-sanctuary,” said the old man.

“That’s right,” said Gavin, patience thinning slightly.

“You can stay at the Government Rest-House Bungalows.”

“Really?” said Gavin, eyebrows raising slightly. The old man continued, matter-of-factly.

“You will need an official request form available only from Madras. It will take you about one month to get it.”

“What if we just roll up unannounced?” said Gavin, now very curious.

“No problem, just give them some lame excuse.”

The old man seemed to be in the know. We had one day to come up with a lame excuse. By the next morning the best we could think of was to enter a plea for compassion. On the strength of that we loaded the bags onto the bikes, waved goodbye to a small but enthusiastic farewell party at the Ramakrishna Lodge, and rumbled off in an easterly direction. For this stretch of the journey the actual route was being finalized largely by guesswork due to the uncertainty of maps and absence of main roads.

An hour later we found ourselves at a small village, twenty kilometers down an ever narrowing and increasingly more potholed track. Central to the village was a main roundabout featuring the statue of a politician in a light-blue suit pointing to the sky with one finger. It was surrounded by a low barrier of sandbags lending the impression that if the village were ever invaded this monument would be the last bastion of defense. We stopped for chai and directions.

"You must go straight," advised a long-bearded man standing by. It might well have been the statue's caption. He gave a general circular swish of the wrist.

"Which way straight?" asked Laxmi. The roundabout offered four posibilities. The man stood up and adjusted his loongie.

"You are going to Vedangtangal is it?"

"Yes," said Laxmi.

"Vedangtangal Bird Sanctuary?"

"Yes."

"Then go directly straight." He moved his arm in a spiraling motion from the elbow up.

"But which way?" said Laxmi getting frustrated. The man lifted back his head and puckered his lips, sucking in air to make a kissing sound in the direction which he wished to indicate. That seemed to narrow it down to three possibilities.

"Do you mean this way?" said Laxmi pointing. The man made a nodding cum shaking circular motion with his head. "Then do you mean this way?" said Laxmi pointing in another direction. The man gave similar head movements but more vigorous. "I give up," said Laxmi. "Let's ask someone else."

A crowd had gathered by this stage to which Gavin addressed. Did anyone know the way to Vedangtangal? Arms swung, heads shook, fingers pointed, wrists spun and lips kissed the air in every direction. The four cardinal points thus indicated. Gavin thanked everyone and turned to Dao, "Your turn."

Before Dao could answer a very old man stepped forward.

"I am telling you Vedangtangal lies in this direction." He stretched a bent and withered arm and pointed with a crooked finger. He appeared to indicate a particular direction.

"Don't ask anyone else," said Dao, perfectly content that someone had been pinned down to a straight answer.

We paid for the chais and prepared to leave. After five minutes of futile attempts at starting my bike a man from the crowd stepped forward and started it first time. We mounted our respective machines and did a lap of the village roundabout out of courtesy to the crowd, and homage to the pointing statue. It seemed to be the right thing to do before exiting on cue.

A few minutes further on a street sign corroborated the villager's directions and gave the distance as forty-two kilometers. We followed rambling country roads through small villages stopping once more for chai and directions before continuing. Up ahead a tractor towed the unusual load of a huge trailer full of young smiling school children all dressed in blue and white uniforms.

"What is your name?" they all shouted in unison as we sped by. We moved on until my bike took one deep pothole too many and the back carrier slipped loose of the one bolt that held it in place. We all stopped. The tractor towing the school children passed us.

“Welcome, goodbye,” they all shouted together as the tractor rattled by. We were on a quiet road of inland Tamil Nadu with a loose back carrier. It meant that Dao would have to carry all of the miscellaneous odds and ends, which had been on the carrier, on her lap. At the same time she would have to reach back and hang onto the lose carrier with one hand to stop it falling into the back wheel. This made the prospect of further travel seem dim.

Just then a man appeared from nowhere. He took one look at the bike and left. Two minutes later he reappeared with a bag full of spanners. They were from his tractor repair shop which was behind some trees directly opposite. In two minutes he had the carrier bolted back in place more secure than the day it had left Madras. He started the bike for us, wished us good luck, and disappeared again.

We continued on our way pondering our good luck and wondering if there wasn’t some higher force taking an interest in the journey. By late afternoon we had accidentally found the correct way to the forest guest house at Vedangtangal Bird Sanctuary. We stopped the bikes at the front gate. Gavin glanced back with raised eyebrows.

“What was that lame excuse one more time?”

“Just say we didn’t know,” I said, which had been perfectly true until the previous day.

“That is indeed a lame excuse,” said Gavin.

The caretaker of the rest house, surprisingly unidentifiable in civvies, was unimpressed with our arrival. The event no doubt interfered with his plans for a quiet evening.

“Do you have a booking?” He played his trump card.

“Booking?” said Laxmi, on cue in rare Shakespearian form.

“Never mind just sign in here.” The caretaker was in no mood for amateur theatrics. We signed in and were shown to two huge upstairs rooms each with adjoining bathrooms. There was one condition: that we wrote ourselves a letter of recommendation and agreed to vacate the rooms should someone else arrive with a booking and a desire to use them. Given our position the terms were perfectly acceptable. Considering the remoteness of the location and the bureaucracy involved, it was unlikely that anyone with a booking ever turned up. It did seem odd writing our own letter of recommendation though.

“This is a bit like writing your own job reference,” said Laxmi.

“It’s just for the paperwork,” I said, wondering who’s job it might be to read the letters of recommendation, all no doubt written by the people whom they recommended. Not that we took much time to knock out a cursory letter. Evening was already approaching and we were keen to get down to the sanctuary before rush-hour for the birds was over. With the letter drawn up and bags thrown into rooms we went straight back outside got on the bikes and rode the final kilometer down to the the bird sanctuary.

“Entrance fee is one rupee, your motorbike parking is two rupees and your camera is five rupees,” we were told by a grinning, mustached man behind the ticket counter at the entrance to the sanctuary. The motorbike fee seemed reasonable but it felt odd to be considered worth less than a cheap instamatic camera.

We had arrived just on dusk and sweeping down from every quarter were great flocks of herons and cormorants. It appeared to be a water-bird paradise with thousands of gliding, darting, singing, squabbling birds pervading every quarter of the sky. Their combined noise raised a cacophony.

In February it was the bird high season. The lake was now in full flood. Come April when the waters would dry up in the Summer heat the birds would continue their journey for cooler climes.

“I’m no bird watcher,” said Gavin, “but this place is so remarkable that we do really need to come back tomorrow morning at dawn before we leave.”

“You realise that would mean waking up at five o’clock, don’t you?” said Dao.

“I am aware that this plan is not for the undetermined, but how often have you seen a spectacle like this?” Gavin waved at the air teeming with uncountable varieties of birds. He was right, we had witnessed a dusk-time scene of unrivaled splendor. Now it remained to witness the dawn at this spectacular place. It would mean setting the alarm clocks early.

Sunrise at Vedangtangal Bird Sanctuary saw three sleep-starved, slightly high, out-of-towners, wonder around the lake. Dao chose sleep as the better path, not having made the firm commitment of the night before. The lake was a hive of activity. Great flocks rose as one while we drank strong chai and ate glucose biscuits at one of the half-a-dozen chai stands around the entrance.

“That was almost worth getting up early for,” said Laxmi.

“Yes, almost,” replied Gavin.

As the chai kicked in we laid our plans for stage three of the journey: Vedangtangal to Tiruvanamali, and the sacred hill of Arunachala. It was already a warm morning and promised to be a very hot day. We would leave early.

Chapter 4 Vedangtangal to Tiruvanamali

February 4, 1998

"This is the biggest and noisiest *'quiet little town'* I've ever visited," said Gavin. He alluded to the now very much out of date guide book which we jokingly relied upon for general information. It was true that our experiences here in Tiruvanamali had so far been of the same busy roads and horn beeping, trucks that were to be expected in most other medium sized, vibrant, Indian cities. This was in marked contrast to the image of a sleepy village conjured up in our guide book. Nonetheless we had arrived without getting seriously lost, despite our three maps of the area all being different.

The full day's ride from the Vedangtangal, bird sanctuary to the east, had passed off fairly well. Gavin and Laxmi were having few if any problems with their bike, while Dao and I were slowly getting used to the quirks of ours. The engine would consistently refuse to start for the first fifteen minutes of any given attempt. Having done so, it would thump away soundly, with a noise to strike fear into the hearts of most onlookers. The bike's suspension also had problems, with the back forks straining under the burden of more weight than they were ever designed to withstand. This extra burden caused the back tyre to bottom out on the mudguard with every large bump in the road. Still these seemed to be small problems in the big scheme of things as the journey was filled with new and spontaneous events at every turn.

Upon arriving we had made straight for the Sri Ramana Maharishi Ashram, a name synomonous with Tiruvanamali and its dominating Arunachala Hill. Sri Ramana had spent most of his life here, many believe in complete enlightenment. The story goes that as a young boy Ramana once had the feeling that he was going to die, so he lay down on the ground to prepare for the event. At this time he made the realization that the physical body is a temporary phenomena whereas the real self is permanent and unlimited by time and space. Still at a young age he felt himself called to the sacred Arunachala Hill. He therefore left home without telling his parents or anyone else where he was going and walked hundreds of miles to get here. Having arrived, he devoted himself to full-time meditation and the people of the area soon recognized him as an enlightened sage. Before his passing in 1950 an ashram had sprung up around him along with a great following of devotees. To ask yourself "Who am I?" was a central point to his teaching. When one discovers that one is free.

"You won't be able to stay at the Ramana Ashram unless you have a reservation. It's booked up for months in advance." A blond German girl told us. "But there will probably be room next door in the Sri Seshadri Ashram. It's less intense there."

We moved in next door. A focal part of the ashram was a shrine dedicated to the guru Mahan Sri Seshadri Swamigal, a contemporary of Sri Ramana. Sri Seshadri didn't have the same popular following, but had led a remarkable life and is generally recognized by his followers today as a saint. Like Sri Ramana he too was drawn to Arunachala at a young age and spent his whole life here. Many thought he was mad because he was known to do things like go into shops and upset the cash till, or disrupt proceedings at a wedding ceremony. Those who understood him knew that those affected by his actions were actually being blessed and they were invariably in for good fortune.

"What do you charge for rooms here?" I asked the dhoti-clad man at the check-in office.

"There is no fee," he replied, "but the contribution will be 100 rupees per night."

"Do you have anyone here to give yoga or meditation instructions?" I asked.

"No," he said, "But there are nine meditation platforms all facing the sacred hill. You can sit there and ponder the mountain". With these words of advice we were led to our simple rooms on the second floor of a guest's wing.

Overlooking the ashram and the whole town of Tiruvanamali was the sacred Arunachala Hill. Upon this hill, the Karttigai, an annual fire ceremony, was held every December. The summit was set ablaze and pilgrims would circumambulate the base on foot. The fire column created by this blaze was worshipped as Lord Shiva. It is also the popular local belief that, whereas Mount Kailash in Tibet is the *abode* of Shiva, Arunachala Hill is Shiva *Himself* in physical manifestation.

"All pilgrims to this place should definitely circumambulate Arunachala Hill or at the least climb barefoot to it's summit," a Hindu devotee dressed in nothing but a white cotton loincloth informed us. "If you decide to climb the hill you may be fortunate enough to meet the non-eating yogi. He stays somewhere near the top, but only receives visitors in the early morning, so you would have to leave at the crack of dawn. It's a two or three hour climb to the summit."

"How long has he been living there?" I asked.

"This I cannot say."

"Does he really eat nothing?"

"This I cannot say."

Despite the lack of hard evidence the prospect of meeting the non-eating yogi of the hill fired our imaginations. Upon speaking to other people at the ashram we soon discovered that his presence on the hill was common knowledge. Everyone knew of him but few could attest to further details. We had to climb that hill. We lay plans for an early morning start.

Late the next morning Gavin, Laxmi, Dao and I reclined in wicker chairs at the airy restaurant across the road from the ashram. A bead of sweat formed on Dao's temple and slowly rolled down the side of her cheek leaving a dark line where it had passed. Four hot chais were placed on the round wicker table before us. Four hands reached for the drinks. That it would be a warm day was certain, and that we each needed strong chais to bolster our resolve was equally certain. We had missed the early morning start but the hill was still there. It seemed to await and call us on. Dao alone seemed less than enthusiastic. A big question hung over her mental and physical preparedness.

“Are you sure you’re up for this Dao?” said Gavin in his politest coffee table manner.
“If you can do it I can do it,” came back the reply.

“Yes but can he do it?” said Laxmi, “or will we have to carry him down on our backs?”

“I’ll be perfectly capable,” said Gavin, “but you can carry my water bottle if you like.”

Regardless of whether or not we were ready, we settled up for the chais, adjusted our head gear and set off on the short walk to the base of the hill. That walk took us through the grounds of the Sri Ramana Ashram which in contrast to the quiet of next door was teeming with ashramites. But now was not the time to stop and chat. We had a mission, to meet the non-eating yogi of Arunachala Hill.

Before going any further it was agreed that if the walk so far had been anything to go by, the hill would be far too hot to contemplate climbing in bare feet. We therefore decided to leave our shoes on, hoping this wouldn’t break any codes of ethics. We were soon to discover with relief, tinged with some disappointment, that everyone else on the hill also wore footwear.

At the back of the ashram grounds the steep track up the hill began immediately. Gavin and Laxmi led the way while Dao and I followed at some distance. As had been feared Dao did not take to the idea of walking up a steep incline on a hot morning with enthusiasm. On the other hand neither was she turning back to accept an early defeat. A little way on, a man dressed in the orange robes of a sadhu sat on a rock by the path thumbing some prayer beads.

“Good morning,” he said cheerfully. “I am The Wondering Monk of The Hill. Have a seat and I will tell you all you need to know of this place.” It seemed odd that he had the whole hill to wonder in yet chose the main track which everyone else walked up to stop and rest.

“We’re with the two people who just passed,” I said, “and should really keep moving.” In the meantime Dao, sensing the opportunity to have a rest, sat down on the rock next to him. “O.K. then,” I said, “lets have a quick breather.”

“In a short while a track on your right will take you down to the hermitage where Sri Ramana spent seven years living and meditating. The track on your left will take you to the top of the hill.” He sounded like a tourist guide.

“Really! Very interesting. Come on Dao the others are getting away.”

“A donation for the information would be most welcome,” said the man dressed as a sadhu. If it was the price for being allowed to continue it would be worth it. I gave a donation, Dao rose slowly to her feet, and we were once more back on the track. We wondered on wiser if poorer, still not quite sure if we had helped out a holy man or been conned by a fast talker. A minute later the track leading to Sri Ramana’s hermitage appeared on the right. We took it and rejoined Gavin and Laxmi in the small courtyard of the famous site.

“You didn’t get waylaid by that guy on the path did you?” said Gavin straight away.

“I’m afraid so.”

“People are more than usually gullible when it comes to the mysteries of the religious path, and there will always be those such as him to fall prey upon innocent victims. You didn't give him any money did you?"

"I did." A small light of realization dawned. I began to wonder if this whole 'holy hill' thing was just an elaborate money spinning hoax.

In the courtyard a natural rivulet of water had been channeled to flow by, providing a fresh supply of drinking water. We refilled the bottles and splashed a little over our faces. A small number of ashramites wondered around, some looking happy, some not, all were silent as it seemed to be the rule for visitors. Stepping through a small doorway we quietly entered into the room now enshrined as that where Sri Ramana had stayed. Inside the silence was complete with two or three devotees sitting in meditation. One wall appeared to be formed from the side of the granite hill itself around which the rest of the room had been built. We too sat in silence for a short time at this special place. Now the forest had been depleted and the natural wildlife destroyed, but the story goes that when Sri Ramana lived here tigers and other wild animals would pass nearby but never harm him owing to the peace he emitted.

Leaving the room we sat down to eat some glucose biscuits which Dao produced as if by magic from her pocket. A cup of tea would have gone down very nicely, but as there was no chance of that we settled for another drink of water.

Dao had an idea. "Shall we go back down now?"

"I think *you* should Dao," said Gavin, "and we'll meet you there after we've been to the top."

That was not what Dao had in mind. She certainly wasn't going to quit now if it meant walking all the way back down on her own. Anything could happen. For one thing she would have to get past the 'wandering monk'. She would come with us to the top rather than that. We walked on in silence following the track which led around boulders, through thick undergrowth, over ridges, and ever upwards. We would rest occasionally, dazed from the heat, to drink, and stare at the increasingly splendid view of the plains below. Near the top of the sacred hill, after a tough three hour walk, we encountered two Hindu devotees.

"Swamiji takes neither food nor water. He only breathes in the fumes of these camphor crystals." The Tamil, loongie-wearing man who related the story produced a small white piece of camphor which his similarly dressed friend set fire to. Fumes wafted a eucalyptus-like scent up into the clean air of Arunachala.

"Swamiji is practicing tapas and meditation continuously. He is dwelling under some bushes at the summit," said the second man. With these words and a few last instructions on how to reach the top, the two men strode off down the hill in the direction from which we had just come.

It was a hot afternoon with not even the small monkeys, of which there were many, bothering to stir. We made a final push for the summit and ten minutes later arrived. Panoramic views of the plains stretched away to the horizon taking in the full 360 degrees. They included a birds-eye view of the town's focal point, the Arunchaleshvara Temple. From this vantage we could clearly see the four towering gateways on its outer perimeters. Inside was a complex system of walled courtyards, bathing tanks, and shrines. It was easy to see why it had taken almost a thousand years to complete. A long term project by anyone's reckoning. It was to this ancient temple, that Sri Ramana first came when he arrived in Tiruvanamalai.

On the summit the rocks were covered in a film of black oily tar. The accumulated residue of fire ceremonies held since time immemorial. The yogi was nowhere in sight. After a brief search around the top with no result we were preparing to give up when Dao noticed a humming sound coming from a clump of bushes. We moved cautiously towards the clump across the hot tar-blackened boulders. From the little grove came the smell of burning camphor and the quiet steady hum of a man rhythmically uttering mantras. Looking in it appeared pitch black as our eyes adjusted from the glare of the bright sunshine. On the other side of a dividing cloth screen an image slowly formed of the dark figure of a thin, bearded man. A piece of sacking was tied around his forehead. It appeared to be in order to catch the maximum amount of fumes rising before him from small pieces of burning camphor. He was chanting steadily and uninterruptedly in a monotone voice with a strong vibrational quality. We hadn't gazed upon this sight for very long before being snapped out of our reverie. A sharp rap with a stick by the yogi on the side of his enclosure seemed to indicate he wished us to leave. Then came two further very sharp raps. We were being sent away in no uncertain manner. The point was taken. Who were we to disturb him who had clearly gone out of his way not to be disturbed. We made our way back down the hill slowly, chastised, and perhaps a little more enlightened for our visit to the top. I began to feel ashamed that I had doubted the authenticity of the place.

"Come on," said Dao, "look how slowly you're all walking!" It was true that the rest of us were all going at a much slower pace on the way back having exhausted most of our energy on the upwards trip. Dao meanwhile seemed to have found an uncanny lease of energy ever since leaving the yogi and was jumping lightly from rock to rock.

"The thin air's affected her," said Gavin. "She thinks she's a mountain goat."

"Are you sure you can make it down?" said Dao, running back up and down again with ease.

"What's gotten into you Dao?" said Laxmi. "You've got more energy than the rest of us put together!"

"I don't know, I just feel light and good."

We never did work out what strange forces had kicked in but Dao was full of energy and no one could keep up with her. Maybe it was the power of the hill. At the bottom a young, bearded sadhu greeted us with palm raised.

"Om nama Shiva. You have met the non-eating yogi?"

"Yes. But he sent us away," I told him.

"Still, you are fortunate to have seen him." The sadhu reached into the folds of his orange robes and pulled out a drawstring bag from which he produced a piece of stone. "Here, take it," he said to me, "It is rare blue-metal rock of Arunachala Hill. When you return to your home keep it there on the shelf and your life will proceed harmoniously and with good luck. After some time you shall see the stone on the shelf and say to yourself, 'Hey there could be something in this!'" I thanked him and we moved on.

"It looks like a stone from the road-works to me," said Gavin. He may have been right, but Arunachala Hill had imbibed us with a renewed sense of the sacred. It's association with Shiva, the Supreme God; its tar covered summit from the annual fire festival; its view overlooking the Annamalai Temple; the ashram where Sri Ramana had dwelt for seven years; and not least its living non-eating yogi, all combined to intensify the feeling of the presence of an all knowing intelligence in the very air one breathed.

The hill had also provided us with a good view across the dry plains of Tamil Nadu and the route east. We would have to follow that route for most of the next day on the next phase of the journey, a ride to the ex-Raj hill-station of Yercaud.

Yercaud itself was beyond the range of a single day's ride. Since the beginning of the journey estimates of what could be realistically attempted in a day's riding had been slowly revised downwards. Anything more than a hundred and fifty kilometers was by now ruled out. We could make Salem if prevailing conditions were favourable. These included the temperaments of the bikes as well as their riders and the odds of not being diverted on the way by a thousand unforeseeable possibilities.

Chapter 5 Tiruvanamali to Salem

February 8, 1998

"That's the last time I go hill-walking for the rest of my life," said Dao, climbing slowly onto the back of the bike. Intentions of an early start had been delayed by a slow rise and late breakfast. This was put down to the recovery process following the previous day's climb up Arunachala Hill. Dao, who had been most sprightly the day before was suffering badly from sore calf muscles.

"Well you will go charging up the sides of hills like a wild mountain goat now won't you," said Gavin rubbing it in.

"At least I didn't act like a monkey every time we saw one," said Dao. "I thought you were going to stay up there with them."

With such pleasantries duly exchanged and bags finally packed onto bikes we were all set to leave at the leisurely hour of eleven o'clock. Our sights were set initially on the little known town of Vallappadhi, a small half-way dot on the map at a minor road junction. From the map it looked like a potential lunch-time stop-over on the way through to Salem, the regional capital.

Two hours into the journey, through a maze of switchback country roads, we encountered a low hill range and began to experience the familiar feeling of being totally lost. We stopped for chai and directions at a small village.

A huge crowd gathered all wanting to know where we were from and where going to, and why on earth we had chosen their little village to stop at. Language was the main barrier with very few of the villagers familiar with more than the basic rudiments of English and our collective knowledge of Tamil being limited to *varnakum*, *nandri* and *sacre elam*: “hello”, “thank you”, and “no sugar.”

“You are wanting to go to Valappadi is it?” replied a middle-aged man to our enquiries. “You can reach it easily from here. There will be five kilometers of rough road and the rest will be fine.” We thanked the man for his directions and waved goodbye to the rest of the village.

The road which our village acquaintance had casually pointed out began as a rough, stony but plausible track, and slowly deteriorated. It was a route which had been favoured by heavy trucks during the monsoon. The two grooves left by their tyres in the now dry clay were so deep that if one of the bikes slipped in, it would have to be physically lifted out by all four of us. This would require a huge struggle, with the forces of gravity not bowing easily to its prize of 185 kilograms of motor bike and accompanying luggage.

The only way to avoid going down one of these fearsome trenches was to carefully ride along the bumpy track running down the middle of the two. Compounding the problem for Dao and me was the fickleness of the clutch mechanism on our bike. A certain knack was required to change down the gears without shearing teeth from cogs. At best it would involve an unnerving, grinding followed by a loud clunk, at which point the spark plug would typically stop firing. This would bring the engine to a stand-still. Whenever that happened the machine would refuse to start for fifteen minutes while it cooled down. Longer than fifteen minutes would make it too cool, and even more difficult to start.

Related to this ongoing problem with the faulty clutch was its ongoing inability to completely disengage the engine. The bike therefore still had to continue rolling forward if it was in gear, otherwise the engine would cut out. While this had been a manageable quirk on the open road it now became cause for undisguised terror, and some hilarity, as we tried desperately to maintain the bike’s balance on the stony, uneven terrain six feet wide. More then once Dao and I were forced to abandon our machine at the last moment as it slipped away over the edge of negotiable track. This would give rise to great laughter from Gavin and Laxmi who's bike was still behaving unreasonably well. Then would begin again the back wrenching task of hauling the machine out of the trench and back on to the medium track.

It took three hours of amateur trial-bike riding, heat, exhaustion, torn shirts, scratches and bruises, to cover the five kilometers of "rough road". Yet still there was no sign of Valappadi. Directions given by rare passers-by were fired out in fluent Tamil, void of any of the four words we knew. Occasionally we would hear the word "Valappadi" pronounced in one syllable, which alone gave hope.

We finally reached Valappadi hungry and tired at five pm. Far from being the tiny one-horse town which the map had indicated it turned out to be a thriving centre of industry and activity and our hopes were raised that we could find somewhere to stay for the night. We rode past football fields, schools, government offices, and a lively market area. But we didn't pass any "lodgings". There were none. The only solution was to stick with the original plan.

We rode west for another hour on the luxury of tarmac until arriving on the outskirts of the ancient city of Salem. It was a town designed long before the invention of the motor car, and now during the jam-packed rush hour its inhabitants were probably regretting its advent. Cars, buses, trucks, and numerous other street using vehicles crawled along slower than the pedestrians who weaved in and out, stepping between bumpers, and in front of bikes, heedless of the danger. Given the conditions, a remarkably short search brought us to a comfortable "lodgings" with friendly staff. We took it. Right next door was a traditional South Indian vegetarian restaurant serving masala dosas and coffee served upside-down in stainless steel cups and bowls.

A late stroll took us through the town's central bazaars and into a Hindu temple where an evening araati ceremony was being held. Fumes of incense and oil lamps filled the air with a sense of the sacred. Bells were being rung and mantras chanted. It was a very different world, and yet somehow related, to the streets outside where buying and selling continued apace. This was a deeper world, a more vital, truer one, which related one's spiritual self to the ground reality of its existence. Here was the pulse of India. The living continuity of faith and ritual passed down through the aeons from generation to generation. Here to this temple came simple people with simple offerings of flowers and incense from the bazaar. But they came with sincerity, opening their minds and hearts to God in an uninhibited show of devotion. It has been said that memories always stay with one in the subconscious even after they have been apparently forgotten. We would be leaving Salem the next morning, subconsciously enriched.

Chapter 6 Salem to Yercaud

February 9, 1998

"Have you remembered to pack warm clothes ready to hand?" asked Gavin. Beads of perspiration were already formed on his brow. Here on the hot plains of Tamil Nadu talking about warm clothing seemed a little odd.

"Do you think that'll be completely necessary?" I said, raising one eyebrow.

"Yercaud is over fifteen hundred meters high. By the time we're arriving this evening we could be glad of warm togs to throw on."

His words had a hollow ring. The hill-station of Yercaud was the next stop en-route, and at 1515 meters above sea level it was renowned for its scenic views and cool climate. All of mine and Dao's warm clothes were neatly folded at the very bottom of our pack. Ten minutes later, after up turning out and repacking every item in the huge two-person rucksack, warm socks, track-pants, and jumpers were on top and within easy reach.

Ten minutes out of Salem the flat "plains road" ended and the next twenty-eight kilometers saw an upward winding succession of hairpin bends. At each bend the steep road became steeper still, thereby increasing the lightness of the front wheel's steering. This was already exaggerated due to the extra weight of the six bags loaded over the back wheel. Most of the journey up was therefore completed at snail's pace as the front wheel bounced around with scant regard for the way the handlebars directed.

Another serious hazard-factor was the level of recklessness adopted by downward going bus and truck drivers. Road codes meant little to those fearless men who would think nothing of roaring down steep inclines towards cliff-edge precipices and then hitting the breaks while pulling the wheel around at the last second to avoid certain death for themselves and their passengers. Oncoming motorcyclists stood little chance in the face of such onslaught. The only strategy to adopt was to stop before each bend in the road if an air-horn sounded. This was about a thirty-seconds warning that another large vehicle was hurtling down and for all those who valued their lives to move aside.

A number of the strategic bends had light-hearted road signs reminding drivers of the danger. One read, "Overtaking Leads to Undertaking," another, "Better to be Mr. Late than Late Mr."

The road wound ever up providing panoramic views of the plains, lakes, and hills. They were highlighted by rays of sunbeams shinning through chinks in the clouds drifting across an endless expanse of sky.

"No wonder there are so many accidents!" said Dao. "How can drivers concentrate?"

Monkeys greeted us by the side of the road as the bikes rumbled slowly upwards alternating between first and second gears. They were not in the least bit shy despite having strange natural hairstyles reminiscent of a sixties Beatles look.

“Those monkeys look just like you,” said Dao to me, “Especially with their stupid hairstyles!” She laughed out loud.

The higher it got the cooler it got, until finally remembering our warm clothes we stopped and put them on. After an hour of upward mobility we had just passed through a huge coffee plantation for which the area was famous, when suddenly and unexpectedly, we arrived. The final road sign before reaching the top simply said, “You Have Been Sufficiently Warned”.

Cool, secluded Yercaud. Here was an ex-Raj hill-station of the first order. The lower part of the town was centred around an artificial lake. Further afield we were to discover waterfalls, hills, an ancient church, graveyards, huge private schools, and lookout points with views of unparalleled splendor.

A short ride through the hills above the lake led us to the Hill View Hotel where we checked in. It had “Character,” as Gavin put it. There were fine views of the hills through the windows, which wouldn’t close. Neither would the broken wooden door, which allowed for a more than ample supply of cool, fresh wind. The old iron spring beds were complemented by equally old weather-beaten, lumpy cotton-filled mattresses and set off with torn sheets and moth-eaten blankets. A cloud of hardy mosquitoes dwelt in the shower room. At least the water ran. It was very cold.

Dao delivered an ultimatum. “We either leave this hotel, or we leave Yercaud.” As the second part of the demand involved carrying out the first anyway we changed hotels. The new concrete hotel which we moved into had clean rooms, comfortable beds, and hot running water, and absolutely no “Character”. Dao loved it.

The town’s otherwise scenic tranquility was at this time being severely tested due to the run-up to the forthcoming nationwide general elections. As a result, opposing electioneering gangs cruised up and down the main road in old, battered Ambassador cars with megaphones mounted on the roofs crackling away to maximum effect. Election slogans and promises echoed all around the valley from morning to evening. They seemed more likely to have the effect of putting people off elections than actually gaining votes.

A bearded student running a South Indian restaurant, acted on behalf of the informal rumour mill. He informed us that Dao was not the only Thai in the locality. Living further above the town there was a twenty year old girl from Bangkok studying catering. She also had a younger sister and two cousins who resided at the convent boarding school. Further enquiries led us to her home in a small housing community at the end of a steep gravel track. Though complete strangers she and Dao were delighted to meet one another and immediately began chatting away in Thai like old friends. Kep along with her sister and cousins had been living here for the past three years. She was now engaged to a fellow student from Madras and planned to be married the following year.

From the outside, her house looked just like any other clay brick bungalow in the area but stepping inside one soon realized that no local villager lived here. The walls were covered with Thai movie-star posters while cute plastic butterflies hung in wavy flight patterns across the room. Shelves of Thai videos filled one wall and on the desk were a telephone, computer and fax machine.

Before long we were being shown the sights of Yercaud by our very own Thai guide. The first stop was the nearby Sacred Heart convent school where Kep's younger sister and two cousins were studying. The school was headed by two smiling Irish nuns, both well into their eighties. They had been living in India for the past fifty years, since independence. The ancient convent, newly painted, stood prominently on a hill overlooking the misty valley below. Together the nuns and the convent represented a small window into the past. They were the last of the foreign missionaries. The younger ones coming through were all indigenous.

“We have completed our mission,” said one of them, “now it has started it shall continue when we pass on. That’s all we can do.” Few people these days could say that of their lives with such conviction.

Our guided tour continued as far as the balcony by the school playground which offered a view of the valley stretching away below to such a distance as to make the unprepared dizzy. Dao’s fingers clenched the rail in a vice like grip as she stared away below and tried to make polite conversation with Kep. Kep and Dao were very similar in a number of ways and both soon agreed that they were hungry and that eating food would be much more interesting than getting dizzy looking over balconies. Kep therefore wound up our tour of the sights by leading us back to her apartment for a Thai meal. This was a luxury for Dao who hadn’t eaten anything resembling home cooking for nearly two months.

We saw a lot more of Kep over the next few days until the time approached for our moving on from Yercaud. Its captivating beauty was balanced in equal portion by spine chilling gusts of wind which blew in off the hills every evening. They brought with them an ongoing background wail of megaphones crackling away at full blare from the rooftops of those battered Ambassador cars.

For the next day we planned to continue the journey by heading further south to the Christian-Hindu ashram of Shantivarnum. It was a centre where Benedictine monks had explored and tried to understand the underlying principles of Hinduism and incorporate them into their spiritual lives. The Irish nuns had known Fr. Bede the founder of the ashram, personally and both vouched for his saintliness in truly living out what he believed. Sadly he had passed on some years hence. I had previously visited the ashram over ten years before when Fr. Bede had been living there. I looked forward to revisiting the place for which I had good memories.

Chapter 7 Yercaud to Shantivarnum

February 12, 1998

The next morning was crisp and clear. It saw us wrapped in scarves and sweaters but, back on the bikes at high altitude, heading down the winding hill-side, all of our warm clothes weren't quite enough. Dao and I tried to cheer one another up with light conversation.

"Are you cold enough Dao?"

"Yes, I think so, and you?"

"Oh yes, for the time being. It'll be tough when feeling returns to my fingers and toes though."

It was our general hope that we would reach the Shantivarnum Ashram by evening, though as we were none too sure of the way it was left entirely to fate as to where we might wind up by nightfall.

Gavin and Laxmi rode ahead. Their bike whirred along smoothly while ours coughed and spluttered in the thin air for most of the downward journey. Views of sky meeting land on distant horizons once more competed directly with the need to concentrate on sharp hairpin bends and steep cliff faces. A man freewheeling down on an old Bajaj scooter with its engine turned off slowly caught and overtook us as the Enfield laboured on with intermittent engine trouble.

"It's lucky we're going downhill or we would have to get off and push," said Dao, in fine form. The petrol gauge dipped below zero as we limped into Salem by late morning and with just yards to a petrol pump the engine spluttered one last time and died. "You've bought a good reliable bike," said Dao again, "It breaks down everyday."

The plains saw a return to sweltering heat. Removing the top three layers of clothing while the bikes were being filled was just enough to correct the imbalance.

From Salem the bike ran perfectly, perhaps to do with the lower altitude. "It's because of the full tank of petrol" said Dao. She may have been right but *why*? I maintained stoic silence.

The way continued south along the main road for eighty kilometers to the turn-off at the town of Narmakkal. Despite the absence of hairpin bends and treacherous heights the journey was no less dangerous than the downward one from Yercaud. Waves of trucks, buses and Ambassador cars saw to that. Their drivers didn't seem to mind if on-coming motorcyclists lived or died, though one suspected they would have preferred the latter.

Narmakkal, unmentioned in any guide book, was noteworthy for a remarkable landmark, a Hindu temple built atop a huge rock overlooking the town. In the coming weeks we would discover that temples stationed atop hills were a common sight throughout the region. At Narmakkal we turned left on to a secondary road, which led alongside a canal for another eighty kilometers on a direct run to the district capital of Tirichchinopoly, or Trichi as it was more commonly called. The huge Ranganathaswamy Temple at the town of Srirangam six kilometers north of Trichi could be made out long before reaching it. We would visit the famous temple later but now, already late in the afternoon, the more immediate question of working out where we were going was, rightly or wrongly, uppermost in our minds.

On consulting the map it was discovered that we had traveled along the wrong side of the canal and had come at least thirty-five kilometers too far. Some traffic policeman seemed to understand and proceeded to give further, wrong, directions. This mistake was discovered by chance when, stopping for chai immediately after thanking them for their help, we met a woman selling biscuits who was kind enough to point out the correct way. We returned past the traffic policemen and carried on, to their surprise, in the opposite direction to that which they had pointed us in. Just on dusk a signpost appeared by the roadside. It pointed the way down a dusty track which we followed for a couple of hundred yards until arriving at the simple, sandy entrance to Shantivarnum Ashram.

The bikes rumbled noisily into the ashram grounds despite all efforts to idle in silently. The place appeared deserted. Even so its serenity and simplicity were apparent. Other than the evening twitter of birds there was not a sound. Ten years before the ashram had been a lively centre of inter-religious dialogue. It was headed by the charismatic Benedictine monk, Fr. Dom Bede Griffiths. He had spent over thirty years in India living out an ideal of Hindu, Christian unity. During that time he had developed a remarkable understanding of the underlying meanings and values behind these two religious systems. He had shown that they had much in common and could learn from each other and he had even incorporated a number of Hindu customs into the daily life of the ashram. It would be interesting to see how things had developed since his passing a few years back at the age of eighty-six.

“Hello Miss Can I help you?” A bearded head appeared from behind some bushes in the well swept grounds.

“Hello. Who are you?” said Laxmi.

“I am Brother George. I am the Guest Master of this ashram,” he said stepping forward. He was a young man perhaps in his late teens dressed in the safron coloured robe of a Hindu sadhu, the adopted dress of the monks here.

“Is it possible to stay for a few days?”

“Why not!” Brother George showed us to some small, simply furnished rooms as dusk drew in around the silent ashram and birds of countless varieties joined in chorus.

“The bell for evening prayer will sound in ten minutes” he said. “That will be followed by the evening meal.”

Food has a universal appeal which seems to grow stronger the longer it is left out of the diet. We had traveled over two hundred kilometers and hardly eaten a thing since morning, therefore it had a special attraction. Brother George left us to get on with settling in, which for Dao and I meant throwing bags on the floor, opening them and strewing things around until the one or two items actually required came to hand. Before long the whole of our small room had been turned into something resembling an obstacle course. With the evening meal so close, this was not the time to be overly concerned with neatness. There was just time for showers in the separate toilet block a short distance away before the bell rang calling all to prayer, and food.

Five or six monks and two elderly nuns sat cross-legged on the floor in the simple open-air chapel. They all wore the saffron robes of the Hindu *sanyasi*. They were joined by perhaps half a dozen lay people for the time of silent meditation. Not a head turned as we crept quietly in to join them. This time of contemplation each evening was a focal point in the daily lives of these people, as it was for devotees in thousands of ashrams across India. I found it difficult to meditate, having come from a full day on the road but, even so, the beauty and peace of this simple chapel had its own strength to which all present were witness.

A few simple prayers and chants ended this time of silent meditation following which everyone filed outside until the sounding of a bell summoning all to eat. The dining hall was also a model of simplicity. Two long mats ran one down each side of the room upon which everyone sat cross-legged. A server walked up and down giving each person a stainless steel plate and a cup.

He was followed by others carrying buckets of rice, dhal, curries and chapattis. The meal was eaten in complete silence with the server occasionally pointing to his bucket by way of asking if anyone would like more. Another server carefully poured hot milk into each person's cup from a big steel kettle.

The complete silence had the effect of exaggerating the significance of any movement which anyone made. This did nothing to help Dao relax. While she had witnessed Thai Buddhist monks eating in silence countless times at her village temple this was her first time on the receiving end. She glanced around nervously at every slight movement which anyone made. The food was a simple South Indian meal of rice and mild vegetarian curries. Following the meal all present washed their own plates and attended a short outdoor prayer ceremony before returning to their individual rooms.

Dizzy from the day's contrasting effects of alertness and sleepiness, noise and silence, hunger and being fed, Dao and I wondered back to our little cell. Its single dim light bulb left the room in a continual state of semi-darkness which only daylight would relieve. It made no difference to either of us, both asleep and worlds away.

****

"Is this tea or coffee?" asked Laxmi, early the next morning, having taken a sip from her aluminum ashram cup.

"Barring forensic analysis we may never know," said Gavin.

"Whatever it is, it's not very addictive."

Mornings started early at the ashram with a five o'clock wake up bell. Following mass in the chapel and a morning meal a dozen or so people now gathered around the ashram's social focal-point, a hot drinks urn. The urn itself stood in the centre of a circular roofed open-air building with a low wall around the outside acting as one long round bench. The luke-warm, very sweet drink would be sending no one into withdrawal symptoms.

The ashram inhabitants numbered about eight monks and three nuns, of which one was French and looked to be in her eighties. The visitors other than ourselves were two men, an Englishman, of about fifty years old whose name we learned was John and claimed to be Buddhist, and a younger Swiss man who came here so regularly that he had taken up residency in the nearby village.

The ashram itself was beautifully situated among coconut, banana and mango trees. The extended grounds stretched to the banks of the broad Cauvery River, flowing gently by on a wide sandy stretch of beach less than 500 meters from the ashram buildings. It was said by the monks that in the past the river had flooded so badly that the ashram itself had to be evacuated.

We spent three peaceful days at the ashram. Our daily routine was to rise at five a.m. shower, and stumble around in the dark until first light and the song of countless birds. At six o'clock there would be morning meditation in the simple roofed but otherwise open-air chapel. This was followed by mass, breakfast, and morning drinks at around ten o'clock. Following warm drinks at the urn and social good mornings we would wonder over to the motorbikes, and roll them quietly out of the ashram grounds so as not to disturb the serenity. Then we would start them up in a flurry of dust and smoke, and set off on exploratory tours of the surrounding area. In this way we found three ancient Hindu temples each set atop hills and accessible only by climbing long, steep flights of steps. Designed and built hundreds of years ago they remained fully functional. Temple priests performed *araati* before the shrines and monkeys would swing down into the temple grounds to be fed bananas offered by worshipers.

One of the countless curious offshoots of the Hindu system of temple worship seemed to be this semi-dependence of man and animal in a live and let live relationship. Hindus generally are vegetarians and the sacredness of animal life is ingrained very deeply in Hindu mythology. Hanuman the monkey-man is the greatest devotee of Rama, therefore monkeys are sacred. Ganesh the elephant-man, a son of Shiva is probably one of the most popular of the Hindu deities as the giver of knowledge and remover of obstacles. A number of Vishnu's incarnations are also represented in the form of animals such as a fish and a lion. Then there is the sacred cow, associated with Krishna, who was a cow-herd boy, and there are many other sacred animals. This sense of the sacred carries over into the land and plants and not very much gets left out. The overall effect is to impress upon the mind and emotions the imminence of God in everything giving a sense of the sacred throughout one's daily life. Again, in Hindu systems of meditation, the very air which one breathes is perceived as sacred. Each breath carries with it the life force by which God sustains us and by which one realizes unity with The Supreme.

Returning by late afternoons we would once more join the prayer and meditation sessions. I felt in a strong sense that the peace and serenity of the ashram during these evening prayer and meditation sessions had a simple purity lacking in the outside world that we need to rediscover and bring with us again into the rhythms of daily life.

Chapter 8 Shantivarnum to Trichchinopoly

16 February 1998

The morning of our departure arrived. We each had the sense that we would be leaving behind a world of timeless tranquility for a far less meaningful one of noise, hustle and bustle.

"It is my duty to pray for all the guests when they leave here, for a safe journey. I will pray for you." Brother John's words were reassuring. He was the youngest of the brothers and always had an air of well-being. We would be safe, for the next stage of the journey at least.

“We are only going as far as Trichi Today,” I said to Brother John in answer to his enquiries.

“Trichi is the hottest place in India,” was his only reply.

We stood around the hot drinks urn saying final goodbyes to the ashram residents. We had received the kindest hospitality throughout our stay. The ashram still remained simple, holy and uncluttered by the encroachments of superficial distractions from the outside world.

“How long do you plan to be here?” I asked Brother John as we took photos together before leaving.

“I will be here forever,” he said.

“That should solve a lot of problems,” said Gavin later as we walked over to the bikes. “No unnecessary time wasted on wondering where to go next.” It was one problem which we were yet to solve.

It was almost a living example of the Gita’s teaching on being content with one’s station in life. The ideal was to do one’s work and to have no desire to seek reward beyond that. Thereby one discovers a deep sense of contentment with one’s place in relation to the world and to God.

Today we were travelling only as far as Trichi, an hour away. We hoped to visit its famous Rock Fort, with Ganesh temple set high atop a rock overlooking the town and surrounding area. We also wanted to visit the Ranganathaswami Temple, the ancient pilgrimage site to the north of Trichi which we had glimpsed from the road three days earlier.

The road wound back along the irrigation canal which we had earlier followed. By early afternoon the huge temple gateways were once more clearly in view though still a good nine or ten kilometers off. A right hand turn led across a wide bridge spanning the Kaveri River and immediately we were engulfed in Trichi's sea of humanity.

Right in the centre of town the eighty meter high Rock Fort couldn't be missed. We stopped to gaze up at the Ganesh temple at the top surrounded by nothing but a deep blue sky. It would be another steep ascent but no trip to Trichi would be complete without climbing to the top.

"We'll see if we can find a hotel if you stay here with the bikes," shouted Gavin above the noise of the traffic. Gavin and Laxmi proceeded on foot around the block while Dao and I wondered down to the end of the busy lane. It specialised in small make-shift foreign goods shops selling Japanese walkmans and imported soaps. Despite the heat we stopped for a much needed glass of chai at the end of the row of shops. Brother John was right about one thing, this had to be the hottest place in India. It was a very warm day and the heat had put us both into a state of semi-drugged lethargy. We sat down on some steps to finish our chai and then wondered back to the bikes to wait.

Half an hour later Gavin and Laxmi returned. They had walked right around the huge block and had found a hotel next to the tea stall at the end of the street. Dao and I had been drinking chai and sitting on its front steps without noticing it. It was indeed a warm day.

"I don't think you'll like the hotel room Dao," said Gavin, with a cunning grin. "It has cable TV, attached bathrooms, and views from the window overlooking the Rock Fort."

We took the room. Dao hardly glanced at the view once, but managed okay with the TV. She had worked out how to use it before unpacking the bags. Other than short excursions to a nearby restaurant Dao spent most of the next three days in Trichi watching cable TV. There was no remote control devise which presented a small problem but lying on the bed and watching one channel at a time seemed to be the answer.

The following day we paid a visit to the huge Sri Ranganathswarmy Temple of Sriranganputnam. This ancient Vishnu temple was one of the biggest and most complex in South India. It encompassed sixty hectares including courtyards, streets, shops, halls, shrines, and bathing tanks. People hustled, bought, sold, and bartered. Splendid artworks abounded on gateways, walls, and pillars in each direction. A little girl borrowed our binoculars to gaze up in awe at the fine work and colours of some distant carved images. Though she had been born and brought up within the temple grounds this was probably the first time she had witnessed those distant gods in such close proximity.

The temple's main shrine was dedicated to Vishnu, as Ranganatha, lying on and supported by Adisesha, the mythical snake. Vishnu lay in serenity undisturbed amidst the primordial ocean of existence. Here again were found ourselves asking who was Vishnu, and why had this whole magnificent temple been built around this concept of a god lying on a snake in a pool of water? In one way it was a moving image of God's other-worldliness in another it was a powerful expression of His imminence in all creation. The image may be worshipped as God. It is understood to be an image, but it is also understood that God is imminent in all creation including in the image. The image is from God and it also represents Him and is therefore worthy of the greatest veneration. The snake represented spiritual energy, latent in mankind, but of which it is the duty of every sincere spiritual aspirant to try to arouse. In so doing one discovers the eternal depth of one's own being in oneness with The Supreme Reality. This, as I came to understand it, is the goal of yoga and the ultimate goal of Hindu spiritual endeavor.

We left the temple in search of more earthly concerns such as food and an afternoon nap, but evening found us all once more at another temple. As dutiful tourists the mandatory trek to the Ganesh temple at the summit of the Rock Fort was completed.

Hundreds of other people also had the same idea. The Rock was open to all, and we met a large number of Moslems climbing the stairs to the top alongside the Hindus. From the top the view of the city lights and the surrounding area, as good views do, more than compensated for the steep climb up. What draws people to the tops of hills? The views, the splendour, the peace of God in unsophisticated nature? Perhaps that is why people climb hills and why mankind has always been moved to build shrines and temples on their summits.

Chapter 9 Trichchinopoly to Madurai

20 February, 1998

"We *must* see the Sri Meenakshi Temple in Madurai. It is one of the biggest and most spectacular temples in Southern India." I think I managed to convince everyone.

"It's the next logical stop on the way to the East coast," said Laxmi. "Lets hope the bikes still start."

A three day rest in Trichi had done wonders for the bikes. Both seemed to be running well now following some routine tinkering at a mechanic's shop. Such outings had so far been mandatory on all visits to large towns and small. By eleven o'clock the next morning we were ready to continue what was becoming a temple-cum-mechanic's-tour of South India. The bikes both started after only a couple of attempts. Then we spent the next hour riding back and forth among side roads on the outskirts of the city, trying to find the correct route out of town for Madurai.

Madurai, a large, historic city, famed for its huge Sri Meenakshmi temple, could not be missed on any tour of South India, and it fitted in perfectly with our planned route to the east.

The road to Madurai itself was not without its ups downs. Having finally found the correct road out of town both bikes took the opportunity to break down. Gavin's had a recurring tappets problem while ours was the clutch. A stop at a roadside mechanic's sorted out both problems while the four of us ordered up chai from a nearby stand and took bets on whether or not we would make it to Madurai that day.

With the bikes patched up the journey continued on for just over a hundred kilometers down a secondary road winding past fields and villages. Along the horizon appeared long, jagged rock formations running for mile after mile. Surely one of those peaks would have a temple on it. We scanned ridge after ridge and sure enough there on a distant peak was a glimmering temple roof. How one might get up to it remained a mystery. There appeared to be no roads or tracks and climbing looked the only option. Still it made little difference to us, we were on our way to Madurai and detours up the sides of mountains to distant temples would have to wait for another day.

Just on dusk and a hundred miles from Trichi we had almost made our destination. We found ourselves in a traffic jam on the outskirts of Madurai with, a heat to match Trichi. The weather was our least concern though. Not having eaten a thing since before setting out that morning we were all more than a little hungry. There was only one thing between us and food: the traffic and the need to find a hotel before it got too dark to see the holes in the road.

Arriving at what appeared to be a fairly central intersection, judging by the complete traffic chaos, Gavin and Laxmi once again offered to go by foot on an exploratory lap of the block.

“Send a search party if we don't return in three days,” said Gavin, as they walked off into the dusty haze.

They returned sooner then expected and with the good news of having found lodgings. Shortly after we were checking in to the Devi Hotel where everyone we spoke to wanted a tip, including a man standing outside who wasn't even working there. With bags unloaded into rooms there was still one observance which simply had to be made before going to eat, a climb up the stairs to the sixth floor rooftop to look out over the huge Western Gate of the Sri Meenakshi temple. It was covered in hundreds of uniquely sculptured figures from Hindu mythology. The temple's Southern Gate was even taller and more elaborately designed but we would have to wait until the next day before going once around the temple to discover that.

Formalities over, bags thrown in rooms and view duly observed, there was only one thing to do. We went back out into the overcrowded street in search of a good South Indian restaurant. Being a busy street in South India it didn't prove difficult.

Madurai had the feel of a city with ancient roots. It was already a large city in the 3rd century BC and had been growing ever since. Its vibrant crowds and continuity of tradition surged on without rest. Just being there it was difficult not to get caught up in the whole festive atmosphere with processions, parades and bands passing by in almost every direction. It affected Dao so much that the next morning she decided to go in search of a traditional sawa kamez. Sawa kamez shops were on every corner. We found one and stepped inside, to behold sawa kamezes of every fabric and colour and for every occasion.

"Can I help you sir?" said one of the two female shop assistants, both of whom were tall, slender and perfectly dressed in colourful sawa kamezes.

Gavin was spellbound. "Yes I want to buy a sawa kamez." It would have been a disturbing sight to see Gavin wondering around Madurai in women's clothing whatever the colour. "I mean she does."

The shop assistant turned towards Dao. Thirty minutes later Dao managed to procure a pink sawa kamez of light cotton, complete with matching scarf. Now she was ready to mingle into the crowds unnoticed. That would still prove difficult being with a group of strangely dressed foreigners from distant lands, but it was a good first step.

No trip to Madurai would be complete without a tour of the Sri Manakshi temple. Ours began with a visit to a chai stall directly opposite the temple's western gate.

"Four teas please. One 'Sucre illaima', I held up four fingers and then one for dramatic emphasis. My attempted Tamil for 'no sugar' always raised an eyebrow and a smile. The chai stand owner took all this in his stride.

"One tea without," he called over to his assistant.

"...Sugar" I said, feeling it was somehow important to actually say the crucial word. Of course it wasn't. He looked at me pitifully.

"Take it!" he said abruptly, producing a glass of hot, sugarless chai. A moment later three more glasses of chai appeared, sweetened. They had delivered exactly what we asked for. Things were going well. The four of us stood in the gutter, in the half shade of the chai stand and watched the world go by on a warm Friday afternoon in Madurai. A pantheon of brightly coloured Hindu deities gazed down from the gopuram above the temple's gate. We sipped our chai in silence. An occasion to savour.
An old white-mustached man in a white dhoti tottered up and showed us the steel pole by which we were standing.

"I helped to erect this pole many years ago," he said. Up above a maze of wires shot off in every direction. The pole itself had been installed into a lump of now broken concrete. A huge black cow was finding it useful to rub her side up against it. She wondered over to stick her nose into our little group as if to add something to the conversation. It was a big sniffing, dripping nose. She seemed to take for granted the leftovers of the vadas which Gavin had just bought from a shop opposite. Two nonchalant swishes of her wet tongue and they were gone, leafy plates and all. Her nose and tongue next quite clearly indicated that the only other thing she cared for was a slurp of chai and looked slightly disappointed when no one offered her even a sip.

We said good-bye to the old man, who was unfazed by the prospect of our departure, and to the cow, who looked unfazable, and set off across the road in search of the temple's shoe depositing stand. This was an essential first step for all wearers of footwear who wished to enter the temple; which accounted for about half the number of visitors.

At ten p.m. we emerged from the temple. The black cow had moved on and the chai shop had closed. Inside we had witnessed the putting to bed of the deity, Sri Meenakshi. This nightly performance was done to the accompaniment of drums, clarinet, and symbols, along with a lively procession of priests, musicians, and worshippers throughout the temple. Now there was no chai to be had and with Sri Meenashi already asleep that seemed to be our cue. We headed back to the hotel, to pack a myriad of things into bags. Bags which were never quite big enough regardless of whatever was discarded.

"What's the next port of call from here?" asked Laxmi to no one in particular.

"Kodai kanal," came back the unanimous answer. We had been looking forward to visiting the famed hill station of Kodai for too long already.

Chapter 10 Madurai to Kodaikanal

25 February, 1998

"We'll be taking a keen interest in the price of socks and woolly underwear before the day's done," said Gavin, casually strapping water bottles, boots and other odds and ends to the back of his bike. Madurai's morning sun already beat down at 35 degrees in both senses. He had a point though. At 2000 meters above sea level the ex-Raj hill-station of Kodaikanal could be a chilly proposition come evening. That was working on the optimistic assumption that we got that far by evening.

Both bikes started first time which we interpreted as cautious grounds for optimism, and we set off, across the dry plains, for the Palni Hills a hundred kilometers to the west. We rode throughout the morning without coming across a place to stop, even for chai. As morning gave way to afternoon the temperature rose steadily. Still there was no sign of anywhere to stop for lunch. Eventually a small village came into sight which was discovered to have two or three basic looking chai shops. One look inside the smoke filled wooden shacks serving as restaurants was enough for Gavin and Laxmi to reconsider their appetites. They weren't that hungry, and politely declined all overtures, choosing instead to stand out in the hot sun while Dao and I ventured inside.

Feeling carefree and hungry, we pulled up a bench and ordered a plate of their best *roti channa*. This proved to be a bad mistake. Their best was like the worst of other places, or perhaps they had saved the worst for us. The smoke filled air, the stale *roties*, and the watery *channa* sent us both staggering outside to join Gavin and Laxmi over a cup of strong chai in the clean world of the living.

"Good meal?" asked Laxmi.

"It matched the ambiance," I said.

"It was horrible" said Dao. "I'd rather have stayed hungry for a week."

While standing outside in the sun, Gavin and Laxmi had managed to establish that we were probably going in the right direction, which was nice to be reassured of from time to time. According to that assumption we decided to continue. My fourteen attempts at starting the bike produced no result. A young villager, showing a keen interest in the machine, stepped forward and started it first time. I wanted to hug him, but convention called for the more formal handshake and a polite thank you. Then we were off on the final fifty kilometer stretch to Kodaikanal.

The final fifty kilometers was uphill and winding leading through forests and dales. For once my bike was running well which coincided exactly with Gavin's breaking down. The recurring tappets problem forced a chai-and-coconut stop at the well sign-posted Falls View Scenic Lookout. The view, of a distant waterfall, had itself been partially spoiled by a grey, concrete lookout tower erected for people to climb up and admire the view. As it was so warm no one actually used the tower, there were too many steps, but instead spent their time devising ways of taking photographs of the falls without having the tower in the foreground. This was impossible.

Gavin soon had his engine in bits with pieces strewn around the car-park. After a few minor adjustments to the tappets the engine was quickly reassembled.

"Most impressive," said Laxmi, "but will it go?" Gavin gave a condescending look.

"That's what we shall now find out." He kicked it over and the engine roared to life. We were off.

A little further up the hill Dao and I encountered an old man walking beside the road. To pass him we would have to move out slightly into the middle. At the same time a truck happened to be hurtling downhill at a rate which meant death to on-comers. I wisely stopped then, less wisely, lost balance causing the bike to fall over. Dao, by now an expert at jumping clear in these circumstances, landed lightly on her feet. Meanwhile, taking all of the weight of the bike on one leg, due to the incline of the hill, I struggled to raise it. A passer by saw the difficulty and kindly helped get the machine upright. The old man whose life had been in danger, wandered up the hill in blissful ignorance of the whole episode.

By now I began to realize that the bike was in better condition than I was. I had wrenched my back in the bike-raising exercise and hobbling away, began to mentally prepare for a week's recuperation in the chilly air of Kodaikanal. The road wound up and up, and come evening we arrived along with an enclosing mist, precisely two drops of rain and a cold snap.

A roadside clothing seller displayed his wares hanging them over an iron railing. We stopped. His stall was a piece of pavement on the corner of the main bazaar.

"How much are these socks?" asked Dao. She held up a pair of woolly grey socks to the stall owner.

"Ten rupees," came back the reply. It was hardly worth haggling over in that case, which was a bit disappointing for Dao who was all prepared for a good bartering session. Still, at 2000 meters with a brisk evening breeze coming across the hills you don't hang about discussing the price of socks.

"I'll take two pairs," said Dao. It *was* cold. We rode off in search of lodgings, preferably with a fireplace.

Though back-wrenching the trip up to Kodaikanal was worth it. We found lodgings at an old converted house with thick walls, big fire-places, warm blankets and a superb view across the valley. Kodai's cool weather, rolling hills, forests, waterfalls, huge man-made lake and spectacular views made it ideal for anyone seeking to escape from the plains for a day a two. Unfortunately that meant a lot of people. If we were to consider a longer stay it was said that one particular valley turns blue with blooming flowers once every twelve years. The next display would be in 2006. Perhaps we would return for that.

The old spice trading port of Cochin on the west coast of Kerela was our next objective. To get there we would be crossing the Cardamom Hills and the fabled tea estates of Munar.

Chapter 11 Kodaikanal to Munar

March 4, 1998

"You should take the forest road to Munar, it's the highest in South India. You will see wild deer and elephants," said the forest tour guide. We were chatting one evening over a delicious meal in a small hut serving as a restaurant. It was jointly owned and run by three recently graduated chefs from a nearby college. The guide elaborated in great detail on the marvels of the proposed route to the hillside tea estate town.

"Is the road in good condition?" asked Laxmi.

"No. It's almost totally impassable. You'll be lucky if you get through." He continued on without pausing. Further enquiries revealed the existence of an alternative route with a passable road all the way. It would mean going back down to the plains, then west and up into the Cardamom Hills dividing Tamil Nadu from Kerela.

We bade a chilly farewell to Kodaikanal the next morning and set off on the gentle round of curves and bends leading down once more to the plains. At the base of the hill, mirage like, stood a brand new, purpose built, clean and spacious restaurant. There was a huge dining area and a wide variety of foods. We ate sumptuously, spellbound at this stroke of good luck. Then we were off west once more across the wide, dusty plains of Tamil Nadu.

Come early afternoon the first sight of the Hills appeared on the horizon. We stopped for an almost mandatory chai at a small village. Two old women sitting on the steps of their beautiful clay house just didn't know what to make of us but insisted on offering refreshing cups of water.

"*Nandri, Nandri*," we thanked them in our basic Tamil, wondering at the same time if they even spoke Tamil this close to the Kerala border.

Crossing the border would be no simple matter. We were at the very bottom of a mountain forming a small part of the Cardamom Hills. The border crossing was at the top. The rest of the afternoon was spent crunching between first and second gears slowly weaving higher up the side of the hill to Bodinath, possibly the highest town in Tamil Nadu. Bodinath had a Himalayan village feel about it. Built at the top of the hill, it had a view that stretched far across the plains revealing every small hillock and lake to a distant horizon perhaps fifty miles away. The road passing through this town carried buses of travel-sick passengers moving back and forth between Kerela and Tamil Nadu.

"The perfect place for chai," said Gavin. Chai shops were doing a thriving trade. We ordered chai and fried sweet cakes, which seemed to be the town's specialty, and sat on a wooden bench outside gazing absent mindedly at the view and pondering man's insignificance in the grand scale of things. With chai sunk and spirits raised, we saluted the view one last time and took to the bikes.

Immediately ducking low to pass under the check-post boom gate we passed into Kerela. An officer waved cheerfully as though to compensate for not raising the boom. We were after all only on motorcycles and perfectly capable of ducking.

If the steep road up to Bodhinath had revealed the wild splendour of untamed nature, the road to Munar provided views equally spectacular, of a carefully manicured landscape. Tea plantations from valley to valley covered the sides of every slope. Even Dao, calmly non-committal over the view of the plains, was stunned into admitting that this took some beating. Green hills of tea trees stretched as far as the eye could see. For a tea addict such as myself this was a sight of great wonder. I mentally embraced them.

Come dusk, rounding one last bend, the lights of a small town appeared. There nestled into a hilly corner in a little world of its own was the tea estate town of Munar. We were directed to the dormitory sleeping quarters of the forest department building and, for fifty rupees a head, were each provided with a mattress, a sheet, a pillow, a blanket, and a space on the floor of a huge hall to make ourselves at home.

Having staked claims to bits of floor we stepped outside to take in the evening view of the hills of Munar and then a brisk two minute walk into town. The lively night market had a friendly atmosphere and we were soon chatting to some local motorbike enthusiasts over *dal* and *rotis*. Noticably absent was a chai shop. Only coffee was available. A walk once around the town revealed the phenomena was widespread. We eventually found a small stand in an out of the way place that made both chai and coffee.

To our great disgust the chai they served tasted terrible.
Aside from this abnormal preference for coffee in the midst of a tea-plantation Munar appeared to us as the lost Shangri-La of Southern India. High in the Cardamon Hills, the air was clean and the people friendly. Even the drivers were courteous. To the North stretched the Tata Tea Estates across the valleys to beyond the horizon while to the South bordered hundreds of square miles of untouched national park.

Back at the forestry department building we mentally prepared for what could be a chilly night judging by the number of thick blankets the rangers had supplied. Adding to the homeliness was a noisy, colour T.V. which the forest rangers made full use of. Nationwide elections were in full swing and they were keen to keep up with results as they came in. The volume was turned up full even though this meant distorting the sound and having to shout to keep up a conversation. They seemed to enjoy the challenge and chatted throughout the T.V. broadcast. Before long the T.V. was abandoned for the radio. It went just as loud but the tuning needed some adjustment to avoid continuous crackling: a necessity which its operator didn't seem to be aware of. Eventually with election results in, even the radio was switched off allowing the silence of a night by the forest to close in all around.

Chapter 12 Munar to Fort Kochi

March 5, 1998

Three layers of clothing weren't quite enough the next morning, stepping outside into the chill air to behold the splendour of Munar. The town below was surrounded by green hills forests and tea-plantations. The crispness of the morning enlivened everyone with new vitality.

"Did you catch the end of the election results?" I asked Gavin.

"Yes, but as it was in Malayalam it might as well have been the Kerela weather report."

Four forest rangers gathered around to watch the bike-packing process. They were each about thirty-five years old, bearded and grinning. The one grinning the most stepped forward. "That's fifty rupees each," he said, vapour rising from his breath. "Please come again. Next time I will take you on a tour of the wildlife sanctuary. There are tigers, snakes and wild elephants. It is very dangerous."

"We'll look forward to that," said Laxmi.

The forest rangers bid us a cheery farewell. The bikes started first time and we made our way down the steep gravel trail which served as the driveway. It was the most dangerous piece of road we were likely to encounter all day. At the bottom we immediately stopped for breakfast, chai and *vada*. The restaurant owner was slightly taken aback that we wanted chai and not coffee but otherwise treated us with genuine nonchalance, as though foreign tourists on motorbikes stopped there twice a day. Across the road was the outer perimeter of the sporting ground of a huge colonial-style school. A banner hanging from the fence advised passers-by of the forthcoming fifty-third annual football tournament.

Breakfast done we hit the road once more. Fort Kochi was the next destination. The historic spice trading port on the Kerala coast lay two-hundred kilometers due west. The route down through the hills of Munar wound above a bubbling river with occasional waterfalls, not unlike scenes from a Chinese painting. All that was missing were the storks. From our position on the road the whole panoramic view could be taken in, the blue sky, green hills, forests, river, and occasional villages dotted amongst the hills. Gavin pulled alongside to call out above the engine noise.

“Here’s where I’m coming to write the second book.”

“But you haven’t written your first book yet,” I called back.

“Yes but when I do I’ll retire here on the proceeds to write the second.”

Half way down this spectacular route my bike engine backfired one last time and refused to go again. The bike rolled to a silent stop by the side of the road. It was a warm, still, morning with the occasional bird song filtering down through the trees. Gavin and Laxmi who had been ahead soon noticed we weren’t following and returned.

“Hallo. Who are you?” came a voice from somewhere above us, then silence. Again came the voice “Hallo. Who are you?”

“I’m not going to have a conversation with a tree,” said Laxmi. That seemed sensible. Yet voices from the trees continued to call out. Coming as they were from the forest, the question seemed somewhat profound. This was not the time for a philosophical discussion. Gavin and I instead took turns at trying without success to get the bike started. Two young bearded men in colourful *loongies* soon appeared coming down the side of the hill.

“Hallo. Who are you?” said one. Introductions were completed. They were brothers and pointed out their house up above, hidden by dense foliage. They seemed perfectly delighted that the bike had broken down right by their house. A woman carrying a baby next appeared and seemed equally happy. Next on the scene was a man on a bicycle. Following a quick exchange in Malayalam with the two brothers he disappeared back down the hill on his bicycle.

To our great surprise he appeared back up the hill five minutes later with a mechanic sitting on his back carrier. Dressed only in a bright purple *loongie* folded up above his knees he didn’t look like a typical mechanic. A small bag of tools on his lap gave him away. His first question was to ask all our names. Following that he set about fixing the bike sufficiently to get the six kilometers further down the hill to where he assured us there would be a big town with a fully fledged mechanic’s shop. Having cheerfully completed the task he jumped back on the bicycle carrier and was whisked away never to be seen again. The bike was running again. We thanked the two brothers and bid them farewell.

Six kilometers down the road, right on cue, was a big town which had not only a church, a mosque, a temple, and a number of restaurants, but also a motorbike repair shop. We left the bike with the mechanic and retired to a ‘veg / non-veg’ restaurant across the road. We had arrived just in time for *‘meals’*. The restaurant was crowded with people all eating the same dish. We ordered the same. A banana leaf plate was topped up with local rice, curries, pickles and chutneys. The chef knew his dish well and had it perfected right down to the curd water with which it was all washed down.

The mechanic also knew his stuff and it wasn’t long before the bike was running better than it had ever run. Mid-morning crisis over we were back on the bikes once more heading down the long and winding road to Fort Kochi. The journey was one of many extremes. From hills to coast, it was also from cool to warm, and from peaceful to totally hectic. The final run into Fort Kochi through the modern city of Ernaculam could have been likened to a drive through Bangkok in the sense that we soon became completely lost amid high rise buildings and heavy traffic. It was dusk by the time we crossed the harbour bridge spanning the wide estuary, and the centuries of tradition, dividing the modern, ugly, Ernaculam from the quaint historic fishing village of Fort Kochi.

'Lodgings' were in short supply. Gavin and Laxmi eventually got into a dimly lit old building turned hippie home, while Dao and I found a small upstairs room in a house with a view from the balcony of a huge mansion across the road. Gardeners tidied the grounds and limousines rolled in and out through the guarded iron gate. A sign painted in black on a concrete pillar read The Nest. A well feathered nest indeed.

Kochi was famed for its stunning location and the first thing we discovered the next morning was that without a map finding our way around would be no simple matter. It was situated at the northern end of a system of waterways stretching back for hundreds of miles. The complex system of islands, waterways, ferries and bridges meant that anyone from out of town without a map would get lost at least once a day, usually first thing in the morning.

While crossing the waterways the views of Kochi were the picture of serenity. Churches dotted the landscape by the edges of a vast expanse of water. The waterways were not only used by passenger ferries but also cruise ships, trading ships, fishing boats of every size, Indian navy patrol boats, and at least one submarine. They were also home to a large population of dolphins who didn't seem to mind having to put up with the never-ending stream of boats.

Chapter 13 Fort Kochi to Guruvayur

March 13, 1998

Following a good week of idle relaxation at Fort Kochi the journey called once more. The bikes had had their routine pit-stop and seemed to be behaving well again, and we had done most of the things on the general tourist itinerary: visited the oldest church in India; checked out the curious Chinese fishing nets; bought some clothes from a local tailor; ate once at every restaurant; and even learned a few essential words of Malayalam such as, "Please help me I'm lost," and, "Excuse me, where does this ferry go?"

The next stop was to be the Hindu holy town of Guruvayur. Getting there would be a straightforward run up the coast road if only finding the correct route out of Fort Kochi was such an easy matter. After a mere week of daily disorientation we had wrongly presumed to understand the complexities of the ferry system. As Dao and I waved from the boat in mid-stream to Gavin and Laxmi still on the jetty we began to make subconscious reversals of assumption. What we hadn't allowed for was the "general confusion" factor involved in any transition of people from ferries to piers and piers to ferries, which was compounded ten-fold when two heavy motorbikes were thrown into the equation. The result was that Dao and I found ourselves drifting away on a ferry to an uncertain destination while Gavin and Laxmi were stranded on dry land.

"See you on Vypin Island!" I called out above the roar of the diesel engines as the boat pulled away.

"O.K. There should be another boat any time," Gavin called back. We knew what he meant by that and were prepared for a long wait on the other shore. As fate had it we didn't have to wait very long and forty minutes later we were reunited on Vypin Island, a place resplendent with Christian churches and shrines. Now all we had to do was to find our way *off* Vypin Island. It was a long thin landmass with, what we thought was, a single road running right down the middle, from which it was possible to catch glimpses of the vast inlet on either side. Large white herons and other water birds watched our progress as we did the seemingly impossible and got lost. We eventually reached the coast at the other end of the road only to discover that the ferry ran twice a day and it was just pulling out as we arrived. The next one would be in six hours time. A man sitting under a tree began speaking in mid-sentence.

"...however this is the ferry for the South. You will be wanting the Northern ferry isn't it? You will have to return to the fork and turn right. That road will take you to the Northern ferry."

We thanked him for his advice and turned around. There was nothing to lose and six hours to gain. No one had noticed the fork in the road but sure enough it was there when we returned. The road soon turned into a bumpy track leading through green flooded rice fields. The same white herons were still there waiting as though expecting our return. They seemed to watch on cautiously as we took the new route to the Northern ferry port. The ferry soon arrived and following a short voyage set us down by National Highway 17 on the mainland which would take us a hundred kilometers up the coast to Guruvayur. The coastal road was a narrow winding one full of blind bends. It was also very busy with trucks and busses doing a roaring trade. We stuck doggedly to this road for the rest of the day, up and down hills and around one bend after another, swerving constantly to avoid oncoming buses and trucks which seemed to take near death experiences in their stride.

The final turn-off for Guruvayur was unmarked by any obvious road sign. In a country of continuous unexpected irregularities this didn't even raise an eyebrow. We stopped at the top of a hill where a number of uniformed men stood by what was called a "Communist Gathering Booth". They were presumably "communists". Across the road was a shrine cum memorial to the late Rajiv Gandhi. It stood outside a Syrian Orthodox church dedicated to Mary. The communists cheerfully told us we had come too far and sent us back down the hill the way we had come.

At the bottom of the hill another wrong turning led us around a large man-made pool where an old stubble-bearded man sitting on a wall looking into the water was able to give further directions.

“Thank you sir. I will never forget your good kindness,” he called out to us when we were leaving. It had been he who was kind to us. His directions proved good and we were soon rolling noisily into the biggest Krishna pilgrimage site in Kerela. To enter the giant Guruvayur Krishna temple one not only had to be a Hindu but men were required to remove their shirts and wear only a white dhoti. Women didn’t have to do that but were required to wear a sari or at least a skirt. Those conditions counted us out. Laxmi was the only Hindu among us and she had neither a sari nor a skirt.

“Just as well we’re not Hindus,” said Gavin. The sight of our bare chests and bellies in that place would bring all activity to a standstill.” The scene wasn’t hard to imagine. The whole population of the temple pausing mid-breath in silent dismay to take in the sight of two bare-chested white-skinned strangers. What might follow was open to speculation, a stampede perhaps, or at the least a riot. An equally academic question was one of what constitutes being a Hindu. Within the tenets of Hinduism all people have the capacity to reach enlightenment and are therefore equal. Who then was not a Hindu?
The four of us retired to the comfort of a chai stand where for two rupees the owner made the best chai we had come across anywhere in South India.

“What time do you open in the morning?” asked Laxmi.

“Twenty-four hours,” came back the reply. We laid plans to put that claim to the test for breakfast the next day, and we would be looking closely for bags under his eyes.

Chapter 14 Guruvayur to Madikiri via Mahe

March 14, 1998

The chai stand owner's claim never was put to the test as we opted instead for a South Indian breakfast of *masala dosas* at a vegetarian restaurant closer to the hotel. We spent the rest of the morning trying to keep them down on the road to Mahe. The hundred kilometer stretch of winding coastal road was the most hazardous encountered so far on the trip. It was a single lane road with blind bends and hills following one after the other and being used as a national highway by a continuous stream of buses and trucks moving in both directions. The drivers of these vehicles had neither fear of the law nor regard for it, overtaking on blind bends in the normal course of duty. The result was a state of heightened tension throughout the journey brought on by a stream of near death experiences.

"These drivers have neither courtesy nor common sense," said Laxmi during a break by the side of the road. She and Gavin had just had a close call. "We missed that last bus by inches. It's only shear luck that we're both still alive."

Come evening we were rolling into the picturesque ex-French enclave of Mahe. It provided scenic views of the coast from the hills upon which the town was built. A last tinge of Frenchness remained in the red caps worn by the traffic policemen, though Mahe's local reputation lay more in its provisions for cheap liquor. Night time saw the cheap liquor taking its toll as residents staggered about drunk on "Old Monk's xxx". They also took special care not to venture too close to National Highway 17 which passed right through the town. Buses and trucks continued to roar by late into the night.

****

“The world’s most hazardous road,” is how we unanimously dubbed National Highway 17 and come the next morning reached the spontaneous decision to continue our way north by any route other than the coast road. After numerous wrong turnings we found ourselves weaving back up into the hills of the Western Ghats. The road wound along the side of a valley switching back on itself and gaining height until, quite unexpectedly, reaching a bridge across the valley and a state boarder control point, we crossed from Kerela into Karnataka.

As though to mark the change of states Gavin’s bike decided to have an off day. Low on power throughout the climb through the hills of Western Karnataka it eventually stopped altogether by a scenic bend in the road with a clear view of the wide valley below. We gathered around the machine and looked at it blankly. No mechanics were in sight. No people were in sight.

“We could try removing the petrol tank and taking off the rocker covers to see if it looks all right,” said Gavin, as we squatted by the side of the road. It seemed a particularly optimistic suggestion but given our options optimistic suggestions were welcome. Dao had already fallen asleep on a straw mat in-between the bike and a ditch and Laxmi was handing out the biscuits.

“Why not,” I said, diplomatically, thinking that when you have nothing to lose clutching at straws was always worth a try. Anyway it was just far fetched enough to work. An hour and a half later we were knocking the final bolt into place through the petrol tank mounting, having pulled everything apart and, hopefully, having put it back together again in the right order. A passer by stopped. He was a mechanic. Too late to help, except in bashing that last bolt into place. Then to everyone’s surprise the bike started first time. We thanked the mechanic who was on his way downhill, and we continued on our way, which was uphill. To our great surprise Gavin’s bike made it all the way up the hill to the Coorg region on the Deccan Plateau and the scenic coffee and spice town of Madikeri.

One local legend has it that the Coorg people are in part descended from the Greek soldiers of Alexander who migrated south and settled in region. This story is used to explain the people's fighting prowess, which we had no wish to put that to the test. Two huge rooms at the Mayura Valley View Hotel, with hot water, were too good to resist. We booked in for a couple of days and prepared to spend them tinkering with motorbikes.

Chapter 15 Madikiri to Jog Falls, via Karkal

March 17, 1998

"Karkel?" Laxmi intoned the word in the only way possible to make it sound like a request for directions. The answer which came back in the Kanada language of Karnataka was more ambiguous. It could be interpreted in one of two ways: either we had to turn left and go fifty kilometers or go fifty kilometers and turn left. This disturbing dilemma resolved itself at the next left-hand turning which had a sign pointing the way.

We had already spent the day freewheeling, lazily downhill through the green hills and vales of Madikeri. We had stopped twice on the journey, once for chai, and once for something more dramatic: the chain on Gavin's bike snapped. We had pushed the bike up and down the next two hills before rolling silently into a repair shop manned by a very surprised mechanic. The chain was fixed and all moving parts on the bike oiled before we had managed to down our first chai. Then we were back on track, pushing on with the last leg of the day's journey to the small Hindu and Jain holy town of Karkal.

Riding along the open road the thought occurred to me that the date was March the 17th, Saint Patrick's Day. I wondered what the people back home would be doing to mark the occasion: possibly drinking beer in an Irish bar or at the very least singing rebel songs and wearing green. I mentioned it to Dao, sitting behind me on the bike, to whom the idea of a Saint Patrick's Day celebration was about as remote as walking on the moon. Less than two minutes later we passed a huge Catholic church with its spires shooting skyward. It was a remarkable sight in the remote country area of inland Karnataka.

"That's a coincidence," I said to Dao, "we were only just talking about Saint Patrick's Day and now we're passing a church." The coincidence grew. As we rode past the main gate of the long driveway a big sign over the entrance read "Saint Patrick's Catholic Church." It was the first time I had ever come across any mention of Saint Patrick anywhere in India. Surely now we were going in the right direction.

Hours later with the late afternoon we rode into Karkal. Despite the town's scenic location overlooking a hill range our hotel was right next to the bus-stand, with a view through the window of the side of a building nearly as tall as ours.

One of the side-effects of riding a motorbike all day long was a keen appetite, curable only by food. The lively market area had no shortage of restaurants. We made for the first one and ordered "rice with the lot". Four plates of each were soon polished off with very little left to do for the person washing the dishes.

Out on the streets once more a noisy procession of flaming torch bearers was heading up the main road. At the front was a palanquin being carried by four men in white dhotis and preceded by a drummer boy and pipe-blowers. Thinking we were lucky to see such a lively Hindu procession, and on Saint Patrick's Day at that, I stopped to ask a shop owner what it was all about.

"Oh that!" he said, "Nothing to get excited about. They're taking the deity to her sleeping quarters. It happens every day." It wasn't a Saint Patrick's Day parade, but the closest we were likely to get to one in Karkal.

So far the general plan to head for Goa by avoiding the coast road had gone well. The next stage, according to the road map would be Jog falls, the highest waterfalls in India. We set off early the next morning and before long were wheeling around steep hairpin bends on the slow climb to the hill-station of Agambe. Agambe was so little known that on the map it was marked as being on the plains and before actually reaching the hill there had been no indication that it existed. There were fourteen hairpin bends altogether, well marked by road signs. “Better be patient on the road than an in-patient in hospital,” read one sign, “Take your time not your life,” read another.

A short stop at Agambe revealed a hot, sleepy town with a general store, a chai shop, and an old lady selling coconuts for five rupees each. We did the three things: had a chai, bought a newspaper from the general store, and a coconut from the old woman.

“Your friend came here yesterday,” said the woman. As none of us had ever been there before, or knew the woman, it seemed unlikely.

“Our friend?” I said.

“Yes. He was from Switzerland. He came on a motorbike and stopped here for a coconut.”

I explained that it was a rare coincidence. It couldn’t be often that tourists on motorbikes passed this way and stopped for a coconut. Now it had happened two days in a row. We asked for the directions to Jog Falls, which she had never heard of. She had heard of the town of Sagar though, which we didn’t know of, and gave us directions there instead. The map showed Sagar was on the route. The directions were complicated and we spent the rest of the afternoon taking wrong turns on narrow, winding, country roads. We never met the Swiss man on his bike but could only hope that he asked for just a coconut and not directions from the old woman.

By sunset we were hungry again, but back on track. We had found Sagar and passing through it turned left for the final fifty kilometers to Jog Falls. We arrived at the small village just on dusk. An all pervading rumbling noise filled the air but by the time we had found lodgings at the Mayura Hotel, with a window view of the falls, it was too dark to see them. Our first view would have to be the next day. Before then we would have to be content with just listening to India's highest falls.

Living quarters were more than ample at the Mayura, an old Raj-style bungalow with six rooms per guest. That was more rooms than we had bags to put in them. The hotel kitchen specialised in tea, toast and omelettes for breakfast, lunch and tea. For anything else we would have to try our luck at a make-shift line of restaurants by the very quiet bus stand.

It was at the bus stand the next morning that we had our first real view of the falls. At two hundred and fifty meters high the Rani waterfall was the highest in India and, from what we could see, possibly the one with the least amount of water. The Sharavati River which fed it was low at this time of year and the volume of water tumbling over the sheer cliff into the rocky chasm below was more of a trickle than a gushing torrent. Over breakfast we we discussed plans.

"We *do* have to walk to the top of the falls," said Gavin.

"Good idea!" said Dao, surprising everyone. She wasn't usually keen on such active excursions. Laxmi remained silent.

By lunch time plans hadn't changed and come 4 p.m. Gavin, Dao and I were ready. We rode the bikes two kilometers to the nearest point on the road from where it was possible to reach the falls. From here we struck out into the river-side jungle for fifteen minutes before reaching the open spaces of the river itself. Large and small grey boulders dotted the river making the going fairly easy, hopping from one boulder to the next moving surely towards the top of the falls. Boulder jumping is an art which demands concentration. One mistake and one can easily lose balance, twist an ankle or fall into the river. It doesn't lend itself to sky gazing or even time watching. Therefore completely unnoticed until its latter stages was the acute angle of the sun turning the rocks first blue, then pink, then a darker shade of grey.

“It would have been nicer if we had allowed ourselves another half an hour for this walk,” said Gavin, as we squatted on rocks near the top of the falls to watch the sunset behind the distant hills. The grey rocks we were standing on would soon be greyer and then black, meaning that we could be stuck on a rocky outcrop in the middle of the river at the top of the waterfall for the night. We still hadn’t quite reached the edge of the falls. The sheer drop lay beyond another precarious stretch of rocks. We had already hopped and climbed across many similar ones but to go further, though very tempting could be pushing our luck over the edge, so to speak.

Precious time ticked away as we pondered the possibility of stone hopping all the way to the edge of the falls in the last remaining light. They could be heard with a low rumbling noise and couldn’t be more than five hundred meters away.

“Wait a minute,” said Dao, in a moment of inspired wisdom. “Even if we get to the falls we won’t be able to see them. It’ll be too dark.” She was right, and not only that, we wouldn’t be able to see clearly enough to get back until the moon rose. The moon wasn’t due to rise until 2 a.m. Even if we rushed back now we would have difficulty with the fading light. Nevertheless this didn’t stop us from discussing the question at length before coming to our senses. When we did come to our senses we had a thirty minute river rock hop and bush walk to complete and fifteen minutes of fading light to do it in. It was time to graciously accept defeat and beat a hasty retreat. The big grey boulders were turning darker and more shadow-like by the second. They looked nothing like the pink and blue ones we had crossed on the way out. Even the river seemed to sound louder in the clear evening air as our concentration focused more urgently on the task in hand and conversation dropped to a minimum. Every hand hold and footfall took on a greater significance in the fading light, until the reality set in, with the sunset, that we weren't going to make it back to the point on the bank where we had started.

"This could be time for a rethink," said Gavin.

"Do you mean strike out for the closest point on the bank and hope for the best?" I said.

"Precisely" said Gavin.

In the very last of the fading light we struck out across the boulders for the nearest point on the bank and, reaching the edge, plunged into the darkness of the jungle.

"From here on things should get interesting," said Gavin. We groped slipped and stumbled through thick undergrowth in the general direction of where the road might lie. Dao's voice sounded up ahead in the darkness. She appeared to have found some sort of a path. Fifteen minutes later, hanging onto one another's shirt tails we emerged onto the road, clothes torn, scratched and disheveled.

"So what was the view like from the edge of the falls?" asked Laxmi when we retuned to the hotel.

"Oh! Spectacular!" said Gavin. "The sunset, pinks, mauves, oranges..."

"We didn't get to the falls," said Dao. "It got dark and we came back. It was lucky we didn't have to stay all night on the rocks."

Laxmi chuckled all through dinner and for the rest of the evening as we moved through rooms packing bags for the next leg of the trip on the winding road down to the coast and the holy town of Gokharn.

Chapter 16 Jog Falls to Gokharn

March 20, 1998

"Does any of this look familiar to you?" said Gavin pulling alongside, as we rolled slowly into the ancient Hindu town of Gokarn. I had been here once before, fourteen years ago during the annual three day Shivatri festival: a time when thousands of pilgrims from all over the state converged on the small town. Back then I and my travelling companions had slept on the beach along with thousands of others. It had been a long wide beach with pure white sand. I was sure to remember the way.

True to form, the journey began much later in the morning than had been planned. Following the house breakfast special of tea and toast a start had been made before the lunch menus came out. The thirty kilometer route to the coast had been tough going on a rough, secondary road. Its shortcomings were balanced by sweeping views of the hills at every twist and turn. Reaching the coast we had turned north to discover the fifty kilometer stretch to Gokharn defied all predictions. Instead of the congested, one lane, coastal route which we had encountered further south this was among the smoothest and quietest roads we had found anywhere in South India. The full day's journey totaled eighty kilometers and had been completed in less than four hours. For the first time on the trip we had averaged over 25 kilometers an hour in one day, a record!

"Not entirely," I called out. "But follow me… it will all come back." Three incredulous faces turned to stare blankly. "Well, we can't get lost in a small place like this can we?" I said to reassure everyone while moving ahead to take the lead.

We all knew from experience that it was very easy to get lost in a small place like that, and just to prove it we did. Luckily Dao, who had been on the alert for such things was able to remember the route back the way we had come through the small streets and we were soon on the main road again. It was an old narrow road which wound its way through the town and past the ancient

Mahabaleshwar Temple. This was the focal point of the deeply Hindu town. A sign at the front door read “No Foreigners”, a sign of the times perhaps. Nearby another sign in English read “Way to Beach”, with a small map and an arrow pointing the way.

Stoned and disheveled looking western tourists wondered down the dusty road to the beach. We had arrived. Still there was little chance of taking that well earned rest. The sand was so hot that without shoes it was impossible to walk on. We remounted the bikes and independently set out in search of lodgings. Dao and I retreated back to the main road past the temple and up to a small guest house set back from the road. It seemed to front as a health-care centre. To check into a room involved registering with the nurse at the Ayurvedic clinic at the front. No medicine was prescribed. To pay for the room involved a short walk down the road to a general-goods shop and a complicated explanation to a small girl. Gavin and Laxmi meanwhile found a place, where checking in was a more routine matter of filling out two long forms of personal details, each in duplicate.

Dusk found us back at the beach. A deep orange, hazy sun dipped quietly into the wide sea. Gulls called as wispy clouds turned red, pink and mauve. From somewhere behind temple bells clanged and a conch shell sounded. A sense of peace as deep and wide as India filled the air. Many who have visited this place will testify to its serenity. Here on the coast, where man has worshipped God as Shiva for countless centuries, there is a pervading sense of understanding and peace. Man’s incursion into the natural elements has been minimal and with consideration for the harmony of the elements. As darkness enveloped the beach we picked ourselves up and prepared for our first night in the peace of this serene town.

The next day we found Om Beach. A white sandy beach so named from the shape of its two halves joining together to form a natural Om sign. It lay seven kilometers south of Gokharn at the end of a red dirt road which wound across a wide open escarpment between beach heads.

Other than a few inconspicuous fishermen's huts the only building was an open-air restaurant full of chillum smoking, pancake eating western tourists. Bob Marley music was reverberating out of the speakers. It seemed that perhaps no one else had or ever would match those chilled vibrations.

"We could always get our things together and come out here for a week or two," said Gavin to no one in particular.

"That would be a nice thing to do," I said, dreaming up pictures of laying on the beach all day, taking the odd dip in the sea, and retreating for papaya milkshakes when the going got tough.

Dao looked up in askance, "There's nowhere to stay," she said. She raised an interesting point. There were the fishermen's huts which would do to stow the bags. Then we could always sleep on the beach.

"I think they're expecting us to sleep on the beach Dao," said Laxmi with a broad smile.

"Then again, Gokharn's just fine," said I.

"And we are pushed for time," said Gavin. "I vote we make the final sprint for Goa." There were no objections. Motion carried, we would leave the following day.

Chapter 17 Gokharn to Goa

March 23, 1988

"You are leaving, is it?" A kind, elderly man with round glasses and white moustache spoke in answer to our enquiry.

"Yes, we are."

“Then you must do one thing. Go down this lane and tell the people in the book shop you wish to check out.”

Up until then paying for the hotel room in the morning had proved to be difficult. There hadn’t been anyone in an official capacity to receive the money. This had been in keeping with the haphazard process of registering-in a couple of days earlier. After exhaustive enquiries we were finally directed to the bookshop a few doors down where a small girl standing behind a large wooden counter entered our names in an ancient ledger. She took the money and put it in an old biscuit tin which acted as the till. We thanked her and bid farewell to yet another unique town in Southern India.

The coastal road had been upgraded since my last visit 15 years ago. Then every vehicle travelling South of Goa had to cross at least two streams on hand-punted barges. Now the modern highway ploughed through everything leaving a destroyed environment and quaint lifestyles in its wake. A much bigger shock was lying in store in Goa.

“Think of what tourism in Goa used to be like fifteen years ago and times everything by ten,” had been Gavin’s words of advice as we set off from Gokharn that morning. I had taken his point and psychologically prepared for changes. Perhaps there would be more bungalows around the sleepy beach area of Colva but its natural beauty and serene atmosphere could never change.

Nothing could have been further from the truth or helped to prepare for the scenes of uncontrolled exploitation which greeted us upon arrival at Colva beach. Gone were the miles of palm groves dotted here and there with small villages and gone was the small house in which I had once stayed and dozens like it. In their place were concrete tourist resorts. Others were being thrown up in every direction, with great swathes of land being cleared, leaving just gravel and sand where once the natural landscape had been of unparalleled beauty. Neon signs and tourist shops flourished. Having destroyed the unique beauty and serene atmosphere of the old Goa, developers had mimicked the identity and image of other tourist areas the world over. No longer would tourists meet local people and interact with them in their daily lives. Now they would meet business men from other parts of the country who were there purely for the tourist trade.

“My baby’s milk is too warm!” complained a rich Indian tourist to the shop keeper who had just supplied it at the sprawling tourist market which had sprung up at the entrance to the beach. That was the new mood of Goa. It represented a total change of pace from the unexploited days of tourists renting houses near the beach, doing their own cooking and living on ten rupees a day. Now in Colva there were few houses to rent near the beach. Instead we found a purpose built guest house at Benolim beach and moved in.

Despite our disappointments with the shape of progress in Goa we stayed almost a month. The guest house was in a quiet shady area and had a friendly atmosphere. Five hundred yards away lay the beach. Miles of white sand stretched in either direction. The water was warm and the mild waves rolled in steadily. Mornings would find us in wicker chairs by a beach-side restaurant, relaxing after a swim and having fruit salads for breakfast. On afternoons we would take short rides into the nearby town of Margao or longer trips around Goa to visit the Northern beaches or the state capital Panjii. After a final swim, evenings would see us back in wicker chairs at one of the beach-side restaurants looking out to sea.

So lazy did this lifestyle become that the departure date was continually revised backwards. The old adage remained true that a tour of India should always save Goa for last, for fear that having arrived one would lose all desire to leave.

One very warm night at about twelve o’clock just as Dao and I were about to fall asleep in our room there was a power cut. The ceiling fan whirred slowly to a halt.

“A power cut,” said Dao.

"Yes," said I.

"What shall we do?"

"We could continue going to sleep."

"But I can't sleep in a power cut."

"Why not? If you were sleeping you wouldn't notice."

"Yes, but I can't get to sleep in a power cut. I need the fan to be whirring. It keeps away the mosquitoes." Right on cue a mosquito buzzed by on a slow orbit of my ear. I took a blind swipe and missed. Dao was the recipient.

"Ow!"

"Sorry," I said. I had an idea. We would go to the beach. It was a perfect night, there would be a gentle breeze and no mosquitoes. We would fall asleep on the sand to the sound of waves rolling into the shore. We took one item, a blanket, and headed out the door. A large waning moon shone with just a whisper of cloud drifting past its mellow, dreamy light. We found a secluded stretch of beach, spread out the blanket and prepared to sleep. Waves lapped gently, but other than that there was no sound at all.

"It's so nice out here we should do this every night," I said. Three dogs came playfully bounding towards us and ran in circles around our blanket until Dao shooed them away. "Don't do that Dao," I said. "They're only checking us out. They'll soon be on their way."

"I'm sorry," said Dao, "but I can't sleep with dogs running around kicking up sand." She continued to shoo them away for a little while, then closed her eyes and went straight to sleep. The moon glistened in the water and the waves lapped. After some time the dogs came back and ran in circles around our blanket again. As

Dao was asleep I didn't bother to shoo them off, but instead lay down to try to sleep myself. I lay thinking for a long time and then started to wonder if it wasn't getting much cooler. It was. I sat up. The moon, now a deep red, hung just above the horizon. Slowly it dipped below the waves. A cool draft of air arrived simultaneously from the Arabian Sea. I was sleepy and lay back down to drift away in a cloud of forgetfulness.

There was a warm sensation on my toes. It felt strange, like warm water. I looked up and then sat up quickly. It was a dog peeing on my foot and the end of the blanket.

"Get away!" I yelled, waking up Dao in the process. She sat up and slowly took stock, undecided whether to be angry at the dog, or me, or to laugh at me and be pleased with the dog. She laughed.

"It serves you right for not shooing them away," she said, "ha ha." I hadn't been able to sleep anyway, and now the end of the blanket was wet. We stood up, shook the sand off, and walked back to our room. The power was back on. Dao turned on the fan and we both immediately fell asleep.

Despite living in a guest house we still hadn't forsaken the classic hippie ideal of living in Goa on next to nothing and doing all ones own cooking on the beach. We were just a bit far from the beach to be carrying cooking equipment back and forth, but the front veranda would do. With that in mind Gavin, Laxmi, Dao and I set off on the motorbikes to the Margao markets. We returned four hours later with plates, pots, a frying pan, cups, spoons, and a one litre capacity kerosene stove.

Firing up the stove was a complicated procedure. It involved alternate stages of pumping up the pressure and releasing it until reaching the crucial point when a lighted match had to be held to the vapourizing gases. At this point the whole stove would initially catch fire, burning the operators fingers. Then, as the flames died away a fierce hot fire would remain. After half a dozen attempts it was discovered that by simply throwing a lighted match at the stove from a safe distance ignition could still take place with less danger to fingers.

Gavin was the first to experiment with the actual cooking. Laxmi, Dao and I looked on keenly as eggs were mixed.

“That’s not how you mix eggs,” said Dao.

“No,” said Gavin, “It’s not how *you* mix them.”

“You haven’t added any salt,” said Laxmi.

“That’s correct,” said Gavin, very patiently.

“Are you going to warm the oil first?” said Dao.

“Yes,” said Gavin, patience beginning to wear thin.

“You have to pour the mix in slowly,” said Laxmi.

“I realise that,” said Gavin.

“It’s getting overcooked,” said Dao.

“I’m cooking you next,” said Gavin.

“What is it?” said Laxmi.

“It’s an Omelette.”

“That’s not how you make an omelette,” said Dao.

“Yes it is.”

“It doesn’t taste very nice.”

I had half and Gavin had the other half. It was fine. Gavin didn't do any more cooking after that. He turned the pots, stove and all the other paraphernalia over to Dao, to make Thai curries. Which she did. All agreed they were delicious, which led to long conversations about the possibility of opening a beach-side Thai restaurant.

That would have to be on the next trip. The wheels for this one had already been set in motion and they would soon be rolling to a stop. Laxmi had already made plans to visit some of her many relatives in Gujurat and would be leaving in a couple of days. Gavin, Dao and I still had high hopes of reaching Kathmandu before our limited time and funds were spent.

The day came for Laxmi to fly to Bombay. From there she would catch the train for Surat, infamous for being the centre of an outbreak of bubonic plague two years earlier. From Surat she would take the bus to her family's village for a grand reunion. We rode the bikes down to the airport where there was a fee of ten rupees per head levied for non-passengers who wished to enter.

"Well in that case I guess this is goodbye," said Gavin.

"The plane doesn't leave for another hour," said Laxmi.

We paid the entrance fee to a smug looking ticket man and walked inside. The next hour was spent sitting on plastic chairs commenting on trivia from the quality of the chai to the architecture of the waiting room. The boarding call came. Out came a flurry of last minute goodbyes and exchanges of addresses and, sadly, Laxmi disappeared through the metal detector.

With the party now down to three we mounted the bikes, Gavin's was considerably lighter, and returned to Benolim beach to catch the sunset and contemplate the meaning of life and the strange forces which come into play bringing people into one's life and out again. Dolphins played in the evening light as we sat back and gazed at the ocean from wicker chairs sipping coconut milkshakes.

"It seems we're faced with a choice," said Gavin. "Either we can leave tomorrow for the north and make a bee-line for Nepal, or plan B," he paused for extra effect, "we stay an extra week and then put the bikes on the train."

"That wouldn't be breaking with the original spirit of the journey," I said, trying to think of reasons why it wouldn't.

"What spirit do you mean exactly?" said Gavin, "We're not on the quest of the Holy Grail."

"Let's take the train," said Dao.

That settled it. An extra week of sun, sand and surf in Goa would be no hardship, and two weeks of hard riding would be cut out with just a couple of days on the train.

Plan B was to be no picnic. The whole business began the next day with trying to buy the tickets. That involved searching for the ticket office. That took two days. The third day Gavin, Dao and I took turns at standing in the queue for an hour and a half until it became quite clear that we would be nowhere near the ticket window before 12:30 when it would be closed for lunch. We returned the following day, early, and actually reached the ticket window by 11:00 a.m. It was the wrong window. The correct window was around the corner. We went around the corner. There was only one person being served and then it would be our turn. The man in front seemed to be having a problem with his ticket. The discussion went back and forth without being resolved for the next forty minutes. Finally he left. So did the ticket clerk. He returned twenty minutes later to say that he was closing for lunch.

“No. No, don’t close yet. I’ve been waiting here for an hour,” I said. The ticket clerk demonstrated a well practiced glazed-eyes-yet- long-suffering-look.

“Where do you want to go and when?”

“Delhi, by next week.” Our choices of destination were limited by the availability of North-bound trains within the next week. There were many. All fully booked.

“You can get second class sleepers on the Agra Mail in ten days time. That is the best I can do. The journey will take one full day and two nights.”

“And our motorbikes?”

“You must arrange that separately at the parcels office on the station platform.”

We took the tickets and wondered around to the parcels office. It was immediately recognizable, with a great number of parcels big and small stacked in and around the entrance and spilling out onto the platform. All were wrapped in hessian bag material and stitched together with string at the seams. A tailor, somewhere, must have been employed full-time just to stitch them up. It was someone else’s job, a railway official, to paint the particulars, its owner, destination, etc., of each parcel onto the hessian cloth. He did this in black tar with an old worn out tar brush. A railway officer who appeared to be in charge explained the system.

“If you want to send your bikes to Agra on the same train as you it is very simple. You must arrive two hours before departure time and everything will be arranged.”

The reality would prove to be far from that simple. But we weren’t to know that then. Taking him at his word we happily turned and left for the altogether more relaxing scene at Benolim Beach.

Chapter 18 Goa to Agra

20 April, 1998

Ten days of warm sand and surf rushed by and the time for departure arrived. Dao and I could have spent a complete day gathering accumulated odds and ends, packing them carefully into the correct bags. Instead, as was usually the case, everything was thrown into any bag as it came to hand until they were all full. What didn't fit was tied on to the back of the motorbike. The whole process took twenty minutes. This meant we were only twenty-five minutes behind schedule. We hoped to make up that time on the thirty kilometer journey across Goa to Londa Railway Station.

In practice the unexpected happened. That very morning, a long distance truck driver chose a blind bend on a steep hill near Londa to lose all sense of orientation. He swerved into an oncoming truck. The result, by the time we arrived, was one ten wheel truck in a ditch and a line of traffic winding around the hill for half a kilometer on either side. An old tow truck was being maneuvered slowly into place and a team of people were shackling and directing it. This could have serious implications for our already tight schedule to meet the train.

The ramshackle tow truck clearly wasn't designed for this kind of operation, even when it was new. Still the driver, who was at least twice as old as the truck, seemed to know exactly what he was doing. His truck roared, screamed, strained, and inch by inch, dragged the wreck out onto the road. This was our big chance. A narrow gap had opened by the side of the road and would close again as soon as the tow truck was unshackled.

"Please start first time!" I whispered out loud to the Enfield. It roared to life. "Dao, come on!" She had disappeared into a crowd of onlookers. She reappeared. "Dao! Let's go!" I called, above the revving of many engines of other motorbikes, all of whose riders appeared to have spotted the same window of opportunity. Dao jumped on and we were away through the gap hot in pursuit of Gavin who had already gone. The rest of the journey was considerably easier as all heavy traffic on our side of the road had been held up. We cruised into Londa half an hour before the train was due. That, we hoped, would be ample time to arrange for the transportation of the bikes at the platform parcel office.

One of the things we were discovering on this trip was that things rarely happened the way they might be expected to. Getting things done always seemed to involve a combination of factors which denied logical expectations but allowed great leeway for spontaneous intuition. Such was the case with arrangements for transporting the bikes at the parcel office at Londa Junction.

The first small obstacle was the railway tracks. There was no road-crossing point, which meant that the only way to get the bikes into the station was to carry them across two sets of tracks and then hoist them up four feet on to the platform. Half-a-dozen railway porters sat around at the crossing-point. A spokesman for the group demanded a hundred rupees per bike to carry them over. There appeared to be no official rate-list but their asking price seemed at least five times higher than should have been expected. There was nothing for it but for Gavin and I to go it alone. We spent five minutes unloading the bags from both bikes as the porters looked on with interest. Then, with Dao watching over the bags, and the porters looking on grinning, Gavin and I slowly went about the business of jostling a 185 kilogram motorbike across two sets of railway lines. Ten minutes later we had crossed the lines and had reached the side of the platform, at which point I was starting to wish we had given the job to the porters. Still it was too late to change our minds now, without serious loss of face.

From the other side of the track the porters were standing firm by their first offer of a hundred rupees. For Gavin and I it was the point of no return. There was nothing for it but to somehow lift the bike up on to the platform by ourselves. Together we grabbed a handlebar each and raised the front wheel up to the level of the platform. The porters looked on with amusement. Next Gavin got on to the platform, grabbed both sides of the handlebars and pulled while I tried to stabilize it from the back hoping it wouldn't come crashing back down. Inch by inch we heaved it up on to the platform then, both red in the face and sweating, but with dignity intact, rested it triumphantly on its stand. The porters were crestfallen. They pretended not to notice as we came back to do the same with the next bike.

Next stop was the Parcels Office. After a brief search we found the railways officer responsible for such things. He was sitting at a desk swamped in parcels and surrounded by their owners. Each owner was clamoring to have his parcel secured on the Agra Mail now due at a revised time in fifty minutes. It seemed unbelievable that the Parcels Office could be in such chaos. Surely they had been doing this for years and had ample time and experience to organize themselves. It slowly began to dawn that this chaos was a well orchestrated part of the daily routine whereby one's chances of getting things done were maximized only by giving generous tips at each stage of the process. These included the registration officials, the man who has to be sent to the market to buy the hessian bags and stitch them up around the bikes, the man who marks the destination in tar on the bags, and not least the people responsible for loading the bikes onto the train. There was, we were told, no guarantee and very little chance that the bikes would accompany us on that particular train.

We had paid off everyone and Gavin had even thrown in a new, but unwanted, pair of leather sandals. We were just having a last minute chai on the station when without warning the train pulled in. Dao was faithfully watching all the bags on another part of the busy platform.

“We‘d better get going,” said Gavin. We knocked our chai back in two gulps, paid, and walked around the corner of the platform to where Dao, supposedly, was waiting with the bags. She wasn't there, and nor were the bags.

“She must have found a porter to carry the bags onto the train,” said Gavin. “Let’s find our carriage and see if she’s there.”
It was a long train and our carriage was second from last. To reach it involved walking through teeming crowds all in just as much of a hurry as we were, and all seemingly walking the other way. We found our carriage and mounted the steps. Dao wasn’t there. It was time to think up a plan, quickly.

“O.K. how’s this sound?” I said. “How about if you secure our seats on the carriage and I’ll go back and see if I can find Dao.”

“A sound plan,” said Gavin. There being no time to formulate contingency plans we left it at that. I then proceeded to make my way back up the platform. The crowd seemed thicker. It was as though everyone had turned around and was walking in the opposite direction again. Even if Dao was there it would be difficult to see her. I got back to the original spot where it was supposed that she had last been seen. Still there was no sign of her. I walked on just a little further wondering what the emergency procedure should be in cases like this and there she was, standing in one corner of the platform surrounded by bags and quietly watching the crowds go by.

“Dao,” I called out. “Let’s go!”

Laden with backpacks, helmets, visors, the recently acquired stove, bowls, plates and cups, we struggled off through the crowd and reached the carriage steps just as the train began to move silently out of the station.

Gavin had claimed the seats. For reasons relating to reservations, cancellations and ticketless passengers it always seemed a good precaution to establish to all present that you did actually have a reservation and a berth number. We dumped all our things under and around the seats nodding politely to the other people in the compartment and sat down to breathe a sigh of relief. The train picked up a little more speed as it cut through the outskirts of Londa and then into the open countryside. The sun’s rays filtered through the trees and onto our window. We slowly became accustomed to the rhythmic juddering of the train and settled back on wooden benches for a 36 hour train journey across 2000 miles of India.

****

Two nights and one day later the train pulled into Agra Cantonment Railway Junction. It was ten minutes past five in the morning. The train was Delhi bound and would only be stopping for a few minutes. Dao, who had been sleeping on the lower bunk, called out.

"This is Agra."

"Agra." I woke up. "O.K. Let's grab our stuff and get down. Gavin are you awake? This appears to be our stop." Gavin indicated his comprehension of the urgency by slowly sitting up. Dao and I were hastily grabbing things and jamming them into bags. This process was complicated due to most of our bags being under the bottom bunks along with many other people's bags and sundry effects.

"Have we got everything?" asked Dao, as we picked our way over sleeping bodies to the doorway.

"It feels like we have," I said. Gavin wasn't far behind as we got the door open and stepped down. A light morning breeze blew through the station platform as a number of sleeping bodies wrapped in rags began to stir. We walked down towards the goods wagon where a number of motorbikes were being unloaded. A whistle blew, the goods wagon door slammed shut, a green flag waved and the Agra Mail pulled slowly out of the station. Clutching carbon copy receipts we reached the unloaded bikes. All were still wrapped in their hessien bags.

"Your machines are not here," announced a khaki clad official. "You should try the other end of the platform where the other goods wagon was unloaded. Squinting one's eyes towards the far end of the platform another batch of unloaded goods could just be made out about 200 yards away. We began walking towards it struggling under the weight of accumulated luggage. This weight had been unnoticed when everything was strapped on to the back of the bikes, but now we were starting to realize how heavy it really was.

"You've got everything except the kitchen stove," I said to Gavin in a light hearted manner.

"Yes, and you've got that."

"Dao has actually. I'm just carrying the bowls, pots, pans and oil."

"I don't have the stove," said Dao.

"Are you sure?" I asked.

"Yes, quite sure."

"Then it's probably half way to Delhi by now."

"That solves the question of what to cook," said Gavin. "We'll eat out."

We reached the other end of the platform. "Sorry," said another khaki clad official, "Your machine is not here. You could try the other end of the platform where the other goods wagon was unloaded." It was beginning to look like a cruel hoax.

"Are you two brothers?" said Gavin.

"No," he answered.

"Maybe we weren't generous enough with the tips in Londa," I said.

“You’re right. Nothing less than a cricket bat autographed by Kapil Dev would have been enough,” said Gavin.

“Then you should go to the C.O. office,” said the goods official. Further enquiries led out of the station and down a leafy road of bougainvillea trees to the door of the C.O. office. On the door was written the words, “Control Officer”.

“That should cover just about everything,” said Gavin. We went inside. A genial looking man with a well trimmed moustache and stripy business shirt, and with two telephones on his desk, assured us he would do all that was in his power and we should call back to see him the next day. With this cause for optimism we made ready to take an auto-rickshaw into town.

“Peak Hotel,” I said to the driver in high spirits as we sped away from the station. The three of us with luggage could have probably taken up the top deck of a bus, but crammed into the back of an auto-rickshaw there was breathing room only.

“Peak Hotel is full, but I can take you to a good place,” came back the reply.

“No. Take us to the Peak Hotel even though it’s full,” I insisted.

“I assure you sir, the Peak Hotel is closed now. It is too early in the morning.” It was 9:30 am.

“Then we will wait on the step.”

“Indeed. I think they are closed permanently.”

“Even if it has burnt to the ground we want to go there.”

“Then let me take you to a jewellery shop. My brother is the owner and I can get you the very best stones and lowest prices in Rajasthan.”

“I don’t think so,” I said.

We pulled up at the Peak Hotel. It was open and there were rooms available. It had been over five years since I had last visited Agra and had stayed here. At that time I had been on a boat journey down the Jumna. The owner, a man called Bobby remembered me.

“Ah Bobby. You have finished your boat journey!”

“Yes it *was* five years ago!”

“And now you have returned with a friend, a motorbike, and a wife!”

“Yes.”

“No children?” he boomed, “What’s wrong with you?” He looked seriously concerned. Dodging the question I asked how he came to have a name like Bobby. It was after all a foreign name in these parts. “Well,” he replied, “About thirty years ago when I was born it was the name of a big hit Bollywood movie. Lots of people my age have the name.”

“Lucky Butch Cassidy and the Sundance Kid wasn’t playing,” said Gavin. “That would have been a mouthful.”

The first thing to do at the Peak Hotel having settled into the rooms was to go up to the roof to gaze upon the dome of the Taj Mahal. In the intervening years a low key restaurant had established itself on the roof with wicker chairs and tables. We took a seat, ordered chai, and finally sat back to unwind from the 36 hour train ride. Green parrots and other birds flitted through the trees while monkeys sitting on a wall opposite looked on mischievously. Agra was a city of animals. Pigs scavenged around rubbish tips along with crows and vultures; goats bleated from precarious vantage points balanced upon narrow walls; herds of buffalo wandered by the river, covered in mud; cows grazed on anything remotely edible on street corners; camels pulling wooden carts of grain could be seen lined up at the traffic lights beside the trucks, buses and auto-rickshaws; pack mules were still used to carry bricks in satchels on their backs and even the occasional elephant with mahout might be seen wondering through the bazaars.

The day passed idly by relaxing, chatting and drinking chai, until come late afternoon there was only one place to be. We stood in queue, bought our tickets and went through a cordon of security guards with metal detectors to enter the ornate grounds of the Taj Mahal. It is probably true to say that most people come away from the Taj feeling it exceeded expectations. Its ability to inspire visitors with its grace and charm remained beyond compare. One of its surprises was its sheer size. Because of the setting in large well kept grounds, and its perfect symmetry, its dimensions appear smaller than they really are. Walking around its smooth marble surfaces one's mind soars to new levels of wonder at the unique atmosphere of this remarkable building. From the back one gets a sweeping view of the River Jumna flowing gently by, and the great expanse of wasteland on the other side. Looking up-river to the north-west one clearly sees the striking silhouette of Agra's red fort. It was in a cell of this fort that Shah Jahan, who built the Taj, was imprisoned by his son. The story goes that he had a fine view of the Taj from his prison cell where he spent the last years of his life. With evening's fading light the clear white reflections of the Taj began to take on the changing hues of the sky. First blue, then mauve, and slowly transforming into pink as the sun finally set.

The next day back at the C.O. office reality set in. "The C.O. has taken leave," said the man sitting in the C.O.s chair.

"But only yesterday he told us to come and see him today," said Gavin feigning surprise.

"Be that as it may he has gone on annual holidays. I am in control now," he said with finality. "How may I help you?" It appeared that the control officer had done nothing about the bikes. This included not telling the new man of the situation. Gavin patiently explained everything.

"... and so we would like you to ring Londa to ask if the bikes were sent." The acting C.O. stared back blankly. He wanted to help. He waved at the two identical telephones on the desk in front of him.

"I cannot ring Londa. I can only ring Delhi or Jhansi." We appeared to be out of luck. "Wait, I will ring Delhi and Delhi can ring Londa," came back the inspired suggestion. It was impossible to imagine the number of telephones which might be cluttering the desk of the Railways Clerk in Delhi whose duties would include being able to reach Londa. I was trying to imagine the whole floor of a building, crammed with desks and telephones, one for each station along India's 5000 miles of track.

"So you'll ring Delhi will you?" said Gavin sounding far from convinced.

"Yes. Come back tomorrow to assess their reply."

We left and returned the next day. The acting C.O. had been replaced by his assistant. He tried to send us off to the parcels office, but by now we thought we knew better than to be given the station run around and stood our ground. Half an hour later we were leaving the C.O. office pondering our chances of ever seeing the bikes again when Gavin, clutching at straws, said, "Let's check the parcels office anyway. It'll keep them on their toes." It was a long shot but it was just conceivable that the bikes had been sent to Delhi by some oversight and Delhi had sent them back to Agra. We walked over to the parcels office and made enquiries. The bikes were there.

"Do you play cricket?" asked the duty officer.

"No. I enjoy watching it though," I said.

“I am the captain of our Railways team.” Cricket and the railways. Perhaps the two unifying forces of the British Empire. They were still as potent a force as ever in India even fifty years after independence.

Agra was a crossroads for all points of the compass. It lay equidistant between Delhi to the north, Jhansi to the south, Jaipur to the west and Kanpur to the east. Agra was also to be a crossroads for our trip. Gavin’s plans were to take him on a stone buying spree to Jaipur before turning North for Nepal. Dao and I, with dwindling money reserves, hoped to get to Kathmandu as soon as possible from where we would fly out.

“We’ll keep in touch by email,” I said, leaving on the bike the next morning, following Bobby from the hotel. He was taking me to visit “a very good Enfield mechanic,” for a last tune-up and general going over before the big push for Nepal.

“Take the Western boarder into Nepal,” said Gavin, “It’s supposed to be a top-quality Japanese-funded road from there all the way to Kathmandu.” Gavin was almost ready to go and would have left for Jaipur before my returning to the Hotel.

“Got it,” I said riding away. “See you in Kathmandu.” The next morning Dao and I would begin the final stretch north through India on our own.

Chapter 19 Agra to Tanakpur, Nepal

April 23, 1998

“I’ve ordered you a banana pancake for breakfast and one for me,” said Dao. She was sitting in a wicker chair at the quiet roof-top restaurant. “But as they only come in twos, you’ve got two and I’ve got two.”

It was too early in the morning to ponder why they only come in twos, or why we couldn't have shared one plate. Our pancakes arrived: two each. They were delicious. Fortified with the pancakes we felt ready to take on the road with all its ups and downs. We planned to head first for a district capital of Bareilly. The route would follow a system of secondary roads cutting across the stretch of land lying between the Jumna and the Ganga. By 8:30 we had packed our bags and were already riding out of town. This was a record for us. The usual getaway time was closer to eleven o'clock.

We crossed the Jumna and continued north through mile after mile of busy secondary roads until reaching the mighty Ganga. This was Dao's first ever sighting of the river which featured even in Thai folklore and festivals. Crossing it was a railway bridge, cleverly improvised to serve cars, motorbikes and bicycles when no trains were coming. A train *was* coming. Gates on wheels had been rolled into place by a railway's officer. This duty performed by thousands of such officers across the country seemed insignificant enough but in reality it was one of extremely high responsibility. This was highlighted when every now and then one officer somewhere got drunk, fell asleep, and omitted to do this duty. The result would be another train disaster. The officers here weren't drunk or asleep. The train rumbled across the bridge, the officers wheeled the gates back and alternating sides took turns at crossing with a well devised one way traffic system in operation. There would be no chance now to take a dip in the sacred Ganga. There were still many miles to go before Bareilly.

Eight hours and two-hundred-and-twenty-three kilometers after leaving Agra, Dao and I rolled into the courtyard of the Carlton Hotel, on Station Road, Bareilly. It had been eight hours of shaking over pot-holed roads which had made us too exhausted to even attempt making sense of the fuzzy, out of focus, black and white T.V. in the room. Instead we headed for the markets in search of food.

“What are they?” said Dao, pointing to a pile of small yellow fruit on a market barrow.

“They’re apricots.”

“Oh! We have apricots in Thailand. But I’ve never seen them un-pickled before.” We had to buy some. Dao had her first taste of fresh apricots. She screwed up her face, “They’re much nicer pickled.”

I tasted one. They were unripe. They had one good side effect though. They had probably cured Dao of apricot cravings for years.

After a meal of rice and beans in a run-down restaurant on a busy roundabout we headed back to the hotel. The T.V. still produced the same quality picture, with crackling sound to match. Dao and I were too dazed from the rigours of the road to give it more than a few cursory shakes, which made little difference, and instead went straight to sleep.

Sunrise came with a cold snap, blue skies and a brisk morning air. Dao and I were heading for Nepal and enjoyed a new sense of expectation as we rode North out of the city under the cover of mile after mile of tree-lined highway.

The dream-like start to the morning came down to reality with a thump. Fifty yards ahead a man wobbled uncertainly on a bicycle. Surely, I thought, like anyone else he would hear the thumping 350cc. engine coming. He didn’t. At thirty-five yards he put out his arm to turn right: a path which would cut across ours. Surely he would turn and see us. He didn’t. I began to break as he began to cut across the road. Then, too late, he saw us. The Enfield ran straight into his back wheel knocking him clean off his bike and on to the road. He picked himself up and dusted off his white shirt and trousers. I put the bike on its stand and walked over to him. It was clear that he was upset and ready to start cursing and blaming. There was only one thing for it. I held him by the shoulders in both hands and shook him saying loudly, “Are you ok?” That seemed to take him by surprise.

“Yes,” he said.

“Good.” I turned back. Dao and I got on the bike and rode away before he had time to create a scene. Dao had endured the whole thing silently.

“Are you alright Dao?” I asked as we sped off.

“Yes. I’m fine, how about you?”

“I’m fine, a little shaken but otherwise ok.” We rode on.

We continued along a secondary country road until, by 3:00 pm, we had reached the small boarder town of Tanakpur. A steady stream of people moved uninhibited back and forth across the boarder carrying goods in both directions. The immigration office was an old wooden building where customs officers hung around the doorway with absolutely nothing to do. They eyed us and the bike suspiciously. One of them took our passports and asked questions about our movements.

“Why are you leaving India?”

“Because we are going to Nepal” I said. He remained silent but shook his head disdainfully as though it were an insult that we were leaving his country for another.

“Are you carrying illegal goods?” he asked.

It had been my experience that what constituted being perfectly legal inside a country often became illegal at boarder crossings. It could be anything from a plastic bucket to a Japanese radio, but one could never be too sure.

“No. What particular things did you have in mind?”

“Bombs... guns...drugs...” he raised both eyebrows for drugs, “...money?”

We did of course have money. It was in the form of Indian rupees and U.S. dollars. Fortunately it fell within the bounds of regulations, being not too little and not too much. Our passports were stamped and handed back and we were on our way. There was a short but complicated route to the actual boarder which wound through fields and across a dam wall. Crossing one final checkpoint we were in Nepal.

Chapter 20 Tanakpur to Nepalganj

April 24, 1998

“Where are all the mountains?” said Dao.

“That way.” I pointed north.

“I can’t see them.”

“Nor can I. Must be misty the weather.”

It may have been in the imagination but it seemed that on crossing the boarder into Nepal the whole landscape took on a different hue. It was cleaner, greener, and fresher, with white paddy birds flying by in great flocks as though to welcome us in.

The first stop was the Nepalese immigration office. The duty officer was extremely friendly and had so much information about where to go that he could have worked for the tourism department. Visas were issued at the rate of a dollar a day, payable in dollars cash. Much later we discovered the black market rate for dollars and realized that he had, in the friendliest of ways, made good profit from the transaction.

On leaving the immigration office, with one month visas in hand, a sturdy looking overland camping bus rolled up outside. It was full of Americans who had just toured from Kathmandu and were on their way to India.

"Yeah, there's a few water crossings, but other than that not too much to worry about. Just follow the other motorbikes across the streams and you'll be ok." These words from the American bus driver proved to be more than a slight under-estimation. Come afternoon and many river crossings later we would be starting to wonder exactly how many he meant by 'a few'.

The road itself was smooth tarmac, complete with a white dotted line down the middle. The problem was that while there were many rivers and streams, bridges were non-existent. The first of these river crossings was taken very slowly. It was a fifty yard stretch of narrow ice-cold water flowing down from Himalayan glaciers. The crossing point was cautiously examined from every angle.

A truck approached from the far bank. It plunged into a stretch of the river downstream and ploughed straight across. The water came up past its wheels. Clearly it was too deep for a motorbike to cross there. There was only one thing for it.

"Dao it looks like you're going to have too wade through and find the shallowest route."

"I don't think that's a good idea. Why don't you do it?"

"Because I will be riding the bike following you."

Dao looked at the icy river flowing by with dismay. She got off the bike, rolled up her trousers and bravely waded out into mid-stream. She found a spot which seemed to be shallow enough to aim for and gave the OK signal. I started the bike and edged out into the river, weaving between slippery rocks. The machine inched towards Dao who was in the meantime wading knee-deep towards the other shore. Dreading the thought of stalling mid-stream I kept the revs high and surged forward past Dao and up the side of the far bank. Dao waded through to the bank and climbed up. We had done it!

Just then a man riding a motorbike arrived from the opposite direction. Without stopping or slowing down he rode straight into the river, across to the other side, up the far bank, and disappeared out of sight. Dao and I looked at one another. Perhaps we had been taking it a bit too seriously.

Shortly after that we reached a second river. It was wider, and judging by the water level on the trucks crossing, it was a lot deeper. As we pondered the proposition of plunging in, Nepali-style, another motorbike came along. Its rider knew the route and going upstream found a narrow stretch. We followed. The route led over small slippery boulders and when the engine stalled mid-stream Dao wisely chose to get down and walk. The bike then stalled again and got lodged between some rocks. To slip over at this point would be disaster. Fifteen minutes of delicate balancing ensued with the bike axle deep in the middle of a very cold fast-flowing stream. The engine re-started but the wheels just weren't gripping on the slippery rocks. It was starting to look like Dao would have to wade back in to help push the bike across when it started to slowly slide forward. A few minutes later we were high and dry on the far bank.

The route continued on in this manner for the rest of the afternoon, alternating between the superbly surfaced modern road and slippery muddy tracks leading down to cold, tricky, river crossings. At each crossing Dao would wade out into the middle in search of the shallowest route. Sometimes buffaloes would be crossing or children playing, giving vital clues as to which part of the river to begin exploring. Otherwise we would wait for the next motorcyclist to arrive and follow him across.

At every small village and town a careful check was made for places to stay. Come dusk we were wondering if the road from the western boarder had a single lodge for travellers other than one which had been passed three hours and four river crossings previously. The sky began to cloud over. Our hopes were beginning to fade with the light. The idea of spending the night in a farmer's hut was starting to sound like our best bet. Failing that we faced the prospect of a night in the open without even a ground sheet. Then another small town appeared. Its street lights were already on. It looked similar to many other towns on the Terrai road which we had passed that day. There was one significant difference. Behind a small row of concrete shops lining the main road was a guest house with rooms available.

It was pitch black by the time we had checked-in and unloaded our bags in the concrete bunker-like room. A wooden bed was the only piece of furniture. The room was lit by one dim bulb which sporadically grew dimmer. Water was from a hand pump outside in a dark field of mud and rubble with a few broken bricks in place to act as stepping stones. The night air was beginning to turn very chilly.

"I don't actually need a bath," I said casually.

"How many miles of road, dusty towns and muddy river tracks did we cover today?" said Dao.

"Oh! Not so many."

"Actually very many, and we are both having a bath. Come on. You hold the torch."

We ventured out into the chill night air wrapped in sarongs and carrying towels and soap. It was now very cold. The pump was an old cast-iron one, probably installed in 1901. It needed to be primed with water before it could be operated. A village woman seeing our difficulty very kindly made her way over with an old tin can of water. The pump now had to be kept pumping continuously. It made a consistent loud squeaking noise which partly explained why it was out alone in a field, then came the water gushing out in spurts and stops. Dao took the handle first while I sat under the cold stream and washed. It was the coldest I could remember being in ten years. Then it was Dao's turn. At this point she probably wished she hadn't made the suggestion to bathe that day. Before heading back shivering to our room in the inky blackness I gave the handle two more pumps to fill up a pot of water for tea.

****

The next morning Dao was fresh and lively. I was feeling weak. I put it down to the ten hours on the road and the eight river crossings of the day before. That didn't explain why Dao should be so sprightly though. The skies were still overcast and rain was spitting intermittently as I stepped between the puddles to the water-pump carrying a pot for water to make the day's first cup of tea. A woman had already primed the pump and was using the water to wash some pots. She gladly pumped some for me as I stared on aghast. The water coming out of the pump was dark brown. Not usually a good sign. More concerning was that I had drunk two cups of tea made from it in the dark the previous night. It helped to explain my lack of energy that morning. I could potentially have been coming down with any number of a whole fleet of water born diseases for which Nepal is widely feared. I trod slowly back through the mud to our room to show Dao a sample of this latest discovery. She laughed.

"That is very funny. You have to drink tea wherever we go and now you have drunk that!" Dao pointed to the pot of brown water. Ten percent of it was swirling mud which could be observed slowly settling at the bottom of the pot. I wasn't feeling well.
We went for breakfast in the small restaurant which was part of the guest-house. I asked the owner what water he used.

"Bottled water," was the immediate reply.

"And the pump water?"

"You didn't drink any did you?" He looked up in dismay.

"Yes."

"That water is for washing not drinking! Even a buffalo shouldn't drink it." My stomach took another involuntary turn. A dark man with deep set eyes and a well trimmed mustache walked in. He and a young, slim Nepalese girl had been sharing the room next to us.

"My name is Brian. Like the king," he said, smiling widely. I hadn't heard of a 'King Brian'. He wrote his name down. 'Birendra B.C.' The king of Nepal. They were working for an N.G.O. based in the boarder town of Nepalganj he told me.

"We are ninety kilometers from Nepalganj," he said. "There will be about five kilometers of rough road and the rest is good."

Up until now we had had no idea of where we were. A quick check of the map showed that Butawal the next town en-route was still 300 kilometers off. That decided it. We would head for Nepalganj, even though it would mean a short detour towards the southern boarder with India. In my present state of health ninety kilometers seemed a much more welcome prospect than 300.

The morning's sky was grey with rain clouds and we could hear low, distant rumblings as we rode out onto the main road. Two minutes later the small town had been left behind and we were out in open country. The Terrai road gave views of high green hills to the north but little of the towering Himalayas beyond. A bright flash of light split the grey sky in two. A clap of thunder followed and then came a few steady raindrops. A stick hut stood on its own in a field.

"Do you think this rain will get any worse?" I asked Dao.

"No, keep going, it'll probably clear up," was Dao's hopeful forecast.

Dao's forecast for no rain should have been a clear warning that the heavens would open. They did, but not before we had travelled down the road for a full five minutes. The rain by now had stepped up a tempo from a light drizzle to a heavy, steady downpour. There was nowhere to take refuge except the hut which we had passed five minutes earlier. We turned and fled. The closer we got the more it rained, until by the time we had reached the hut and had parked the bike under its straw thatched eves we were in the middle of a full-scale storm.

The hut, as luck would have it turned out to be a fully operational chai shop, with a number of other people already taking advantage of its benches to sit out the weather. We sat back, soaked through, and drank very sweet chai as the rain poured down and the sky thundered, with seemingly unabashed freedom. An hour later the rain had eased and we set out from the hut in damp clothes into the light drizzle. As predicted by Birendra B.C. we soon encountered the five kilometers of 'rough road'. It was comparable only to an earlier rough stretch of five kilometers which we had encountered in Tamil Nadu and which had taken up the best part of an afternoon. On this stretch however conditions were made worse by the rain and the steep, slippery tracks, and numerous river crossings. The Enfield clearly hadn't been designed with Nepal in mind. This track would have been fine for a light 250cc trail bike and one rider. Two riders with lots of baggage on a 185 kilogram machine was far from the ideal.

The last of the five river crossings on this stretch was the toughest. It was deep, slippery, and right next to a low waterfall. To lose balance would mean losing the bike with all our luggage and taking a wet cold swim to the bank. I wasn't sure which was less appealing and was determined not to have to find out. Dao waded across in search of the shallowest route while I followed on the bike keeping the engine revving high. The current was strong and the stones under foot very slippery. At mid-stream the engine stalled. The bike was in serious danger of losing balance under the force of the current in the rough swirling foot-and-a-half of icy water. Hanging on grimly to avoid losing balance I went through the complicated process of trying to kick-start the bike. It started first time! Under normal conditions it never did that. The bike jolted slowly forward following Dao whose feet were now completely numb. We slid out of the river and up the final steep, muddy track on to the tarmac road once more. Birendra B.C. was sitting in a chai shop waving and smiling as we went by. We waved back but passed up on the opportunity to spend even more time in one morning sitting around in damp clothes waiting for the rain to stop. We continued on down the road west to Nepalganj.

The road was in such good condition that it seemed entirely out of place. It belonged in Japan not Nepal. It did take us straight to our destination though: Nepalganj. We rolled into this western boarder town in record time having encountered not as much as a single pothole the whole way.

The town itself was large and dusty with a lively market area, specializing in miscellany, with an assortment of hardware, plastic-ware, and apples from across the boarder. As we hadn't eaten a single apple the whole time we had been in India it didn't seem to make good sense to buy one now at inflated prices across the boarder in Nepal. Still we had one each and they were very nice.

One ride up and down the main street revealed a number of "lodgings". We stopped at one and checked in. Our room was on the second floor of a small building approached by a short flight of outside stairs leading to a narrow ledge. The door opened outwards which meant entering the room involved balancing on a ledge and carefully reaching out to swing the door fully open before edging slowly past it. Leaving the room was equally dangerous so we tried to keep all comings and goings to a minimum. The proprietor, a good natured chap, seemed to have an extra light in his eyes when he learned of my ailing condition and that we may have to stay a few extra days. The light dimmed a little with my untimely recovery after only one day. Still he put on a brave face and wished us a cheery goodbye.

It was a crisp, clear morning as we set off from Nepalganj for the next major town of Butwal to the west. The first ten kilometers led north back to a large intersection at the main east-west road. Here we turned right and continued east across the Terrai. The bike hadn't seen a mechanic since Agra which was by now many miles away, and it was beginning to show its frailties. The main cause for concern was the clutch, which refused to engage completely. It wasn't very noticeable when going slowly around obstacles in busy towns but once out on the open road it soon stopped operating according to specifications. The result was that for most of the journey across Nepal the bike was incapable of travelling over 40 kilometers an hour. It chugged on slowly.

If it had been cool in the morning by midday it had turned warm and by 3:00 p.m. as we rolled into Butwal it was steaming hot. Butwal was a large town but its inhabitants, like us, appeared to be reeling from the effects of the warm weather, and all activity had ground to a halt. We found a six story hotel, empty of guests, and moved into a room on the fourth floor. It was run by a skeleton staff of three teenage boys. One checked us in, another showed us to our room, and the third brought us buckets of water at regular intervals. The plumbing didn't work.

With bags unceremoniously dumped into the room we went in search of food. We found some at an outdoor restaurant where trees gave shade to the tables. Birds also used the trees and sent regular droppings onto the tables and into any food that happened to be on them.

"The direct road to Pokhara isn't in good condition, but its ok for motorbikes. The longer route has a much better road. It goes via Mugling." The advice came from the semi-bearded man serving our rice and vegetable curry. He was the first person in the town that we had met that spoke even rudimentary English. "What sort of motorbike do you have?" he asked.

"An Enfield."

"Then take the Mugling road," he said with a knowing look. There was no arguing with a knowing look like that. "From Mugling you turn left for Pokhara and turn right for Kathmandu. Kathmandu is 179 kilometers from here."

"Are you sure?" I asked. It was after all our general rule to double check such details.

"Yes," he replied with complete certainty. That settled it. The next morning we would set out on the final leg of our journey to Kathmandu.

Chapter 21 Butwal to Kathmandu

28 April, 1998

The first stretch of road to Mugling wound along the side of a deep river valley. Down below white water rapids thundered continuously, as they surely had done from time immemorial. Above on the far side of the valley, a huge hill reached skyward. A faint dot two thirds of the way up suggested a lone house, though how anyone could have lived up there was beyond imagination. We reached Mugling by early afternoon. It was a small town at the junction of three roads. The way east led to Pokhara and the Annapurna Ranges. With time and money running out we turned west and followed the hilly road to Kathmandu.

Eighteen years previously the Kathmandu to Pokhara road had been a series of loose stones and potholes. The bus journey, bumping up and down around the sides of mountains had been an exercise in self-mortification. The river crossings were momentous events. Bridges didn't exist and every river was forded with due caution. Drivers' instincts had played a crucial role, and the wayside was littered with abandoned buses and trucks that didn't make it. Now times had changed. A wide, smooth tarmac road had replaced the old track. There was a neat dotted white line going down the middle. Fording rivers was a thing of the past. There were sturdy bridges in place at every crossing. The speed as well as the volume of traffic had increased dramatically. Then buses had lumbered along like old buffaloes. Now they almost flew, hurling around bends and down hills bumper to bumper.

It was just on evening as we climbed the final hill in a stream of smoky traffic and beheld the lights of the city of Kathmandu below. Swayambunath Temple could be clearly seen in the distance standing proudly on a hill just outside the city. Not that there was much time for admiring the view. Sandwiched between a truck and a bus in a long line of other trucks and buses all belching smoke our main concern was to avoid succumbing to the fumes. The road began to wind down in more ways than one. By the bottom of the valley it had deteriorated into an obstacle course of ruts and rubble while the traffic congestion had doubled. Within a few minutes we were completely lost in a labyrinth of narrow alleys and roundabouts. It was dark by the time we found ourselves going the wrong way down a one-way street in Tamale. A man in the street volunteered to lead us through narrow alleys and into the front courtyard of the Hotel Pacifist. We checked in to a room on the fourth floor with a fine view of Swayambunath Temple to a backdrop of rolling hills and with that our motorbike journey across India and Nepal was over. It had been just 78 days since we had set out on the Enfield from Madras and we had covered over 2000 kilometers. A few days later in the middle of a thunderstorm we sold the bike to some French guys who were going to ride it back to India. It was raining heavily as they rode away out of the courtyard. The familiar thumping of the Enfield's single 350cc cylinder faded into the distance mingling with the sound of the rain and thunder.

A few days later Gavin arrived. He was full of ideas and enthusiasm for a new project. He had bought some semi-precious stones in Jaipur and planned to have them set in silver in Kathmandu. He would spend the next two weeks sorting out deals with silversmiths and getting each stone set to specification. Then with the stones in capable hands he left for a ten day meditation retreat.

Dao and I would soon fly out to Thailand to resume life where we had left off but not before seeing some of the sights of Kathmandu. We took a bus out to the Pashupati Temple, a huge temple complex built atop a hill overlooking the city. For many this was a one-way journey. Pashupati was the auspicious site for cremations to take place on the banks of the river. When we arrived the final remains of two bodies lay smoking on two burning platforms by the water's edge. Monkeys sat silently looking on from afar, while sadhu look-alikes, as at Durbar Square in the city, posed for photos, displaying their long well-groomed dreadlocks to best advantage.

A few days later Dao and I hired mountain bikes and went for a short cycle up a hill to the north of the city to the Buddhanilkantha Temple. The temple grounds at the top of the steep climb afforded broad views of the Kathmandu valley below. We met three young Nepali boys who were living there. The eldest was probably about twelve years old. They each had badges to say that they were official guides and the eldest spoke good English. They led us around to each of the shrines of the temple explaining their significance. Finally we reached the main shrine, a huge Sleeping Vishnu lying in a large tank of water. Steps led down to the water's edge where hundreds were clamoring to pay homage at the shrine and to offer garlands of marigolds.

The significance of the shrine is that the world is a dream: The dream of Vishnu. Its apparent reality lies only in the way in which one perceives it. When one relates to the body and the mind as hard and fast realities then the senses confirm those perceptions, creating a sense of realness of the material world. Approaching the image of Vishnu's dream a deeper, fuller, spiritual meaning and reality unfolds. The mind and body and senses and all which they perceive are seen to be changing, evolving, seeking meaning, but are not in themselves a final reality. They are passing away along with everything they perceive. There is a truer, more meaningful view of reality to be found at deeper levels of perception. There, where time fades into timelessness, atoms are known in terms of light and consciousness and divisions between thought and form fade into oneness of Being. There, at the source of reality, of creation, sustainment and dissolution, the world of mundane material identity is known to be a passing manifestation, which exists only as long as it takes to realize that it isn't real.

At the beginning of the journey we had visited one of the oldest Hindu temples in India. Carved from a rock, the main shrine at the Shore Temple of Mahabalipurum was of a Sleeping Vishnu. Now at the end of the journey again we were confronted with this ancient, primeval image. Perhaps the whole journey was unreal. It has passed and exists now only in the dreams of Vishnu.

www.ingramcontent.com/pod-product-compliance
Ingram Content Group UK Ltd.
Pitfield, Milton Keynes, MK11 3LW, UK
UKHW051138260726
13967UKWH00010B/3114

9 781300 493259